Faith Pointes

Essential Truths
for
Living the Christian Life

By
Barbara B. Barker
and
Denise Hamilton

D0095655

Faith Pointes
by Barbara B. Barker and Denise Hamilton

Printed in the United States of America

ISBN 978-1-60266-238-4

Contact us at: faithpointes@yahoo.com

www.xulonpress.com

*"Remember your leaders, who spoke the
word of God to you. Consider
the outcome of their way of life and imitate
their faith" Hebrews 13:7.*

I consider Barbara Barker to be one of my spiritual mentors, having sat under her teaching at Briarwood for many years. This book takes biblical lessons and illustrates them with stories from her personal journey of faith. I highly recommend it to all.

Julie Elmer
Women's Coordinator
Briarwood Presbyterian Church

This book is lovely and lively – just like Barbara. Denise has captured Barbara's amazing stories and relational style. She makes us feel like we're sitting in one of Barbara's Bible studies being personally encouraged in our own walk of faith.

Susan Hunt
Author

I loved *Faith Pointes* and read it one day. I felt my own faith strengthened by all of the reminders of Frank and Barbara's powerful witness of a Christ-filled life. Every time I hear Barbara teach, I am challenged and encouraged in my own walk with our Lord. This book has that same effect.

Camilla L. Seabolt
Executive Director
Community Bible Study

TABLE OF CONTENTS

INTRODUCTION

By Barbara B. Barker

Some years ago I was asked to give a ten minute devotional before a meeting. I am not given to short, succinct messages and I pondered over this as much as any other talk I had given. The thought came to me: if I only had ten minutes to live, and I wanted to pass on to my loved ones the most important truths God had taught me, what would I say? What were those things learned from His Word and from years of experience of trusting Him which would provide a firm foundation for their lives? Suddenly those "things" began to come to me and I wrote them down as fast as I could.

Later, I was amazed as I realized just how important and essential these truths were to everyone's spiritual success. Although quite simple, and to most Christians, obvious, it seemed that few Christians were actually living by these truths in their daily lives. Giving intellectual assent to God's great truths is useless unless they are activated and appropriated "by faith." And here was the "Pointe" of it all – *"The just shall live **by his faith**" (Habakkuk 2:4, KJV, emphasis added).*

I did not come about living by faith overnight. Learning to live "by faith" was often a painful, and even frightening experience for me, dependent as I was on the **securities** offered by this world. However, my dear husband continued to challenge me to step out into those places where God could demonstrate HIS trustworthiness. I learned that *"without faith it is impossible to please Him" (Hebrews 11:6)*, and **faith** is simply believing God, as evidenced by obedience to Him and dependence on Him in real life situations.

After giving the devotion, I began to expound upon these essential truths in a Bible Study format, which I taught in many different settings. When my dear friend, Denise Hamilton, heard them several times (as she co-taught with me), she felt led to develop them into a more extensive work, including many of those "real life experiences" through which He demonstrated His faithfulness so often.

The title *Faith Pointes* alludes to the many illustrations that were born of my experience as a dancer and teacher of ballet. The Encarta dictionary defines "Pointe" as "a position on which a ballerina, wearing special shoes, raises herself up for certain moves and positions while performing." As Christians, our feet are *"fitted with the readiness that comes from the Gospel of peace" (Ephesians 6:15)*, which allow us to rise above the circumstances of human experience, not just to trudge through life, but to live gloriously for God.

INTRODUCTION

By Denise Hamilton

My first encounter with Frank and Barbara Barker was at a college church retreat. Even though I don't remember specifics of what was said, I do remember being challenged by their accounts of God's leading through what I call opportunities for faith. After graduation I took a job in Birmingham, Alabama for the sole purpose of joining Briarwood Presbyterian Church and sitting under their teaching. At that time Barbara taught a Bible study for young single girls in her home on Thursday nights and no matter what was happening I was there. She prayed faithfully every week for all of her Bible study girls using large index cards on which we wrote our individual prayer requests. Over the years there is no telling how many cards she has gone through just praying for me alone. Through her teaching and prayers, my life has been permanently changed. God hasn't led me down the same paths, but observing her life has motivated me to trust God in my own seemingly hopeless places with the same kind of unconditional faith.

Right now Barbara teaches eleven weekly women's studies, an eighth grade girls' Sunday School class, and speaks extensively around the country. How many ladies just like me has she impacted? I run across them all the time. A friend in Boaz, Alabama was inspired by Barbara's life to step out in faith and trust God to start a crisis pregnancy center and a non-denominational ministry to teenagers. Another friend from Georgia has only heard Barbara speak a couple of times, but can recite almost word for word some of her faith stories. Now this young woman is stepping out and trusting God for the impossible too. And the stories of Barbara's impact on peoples' lives go on and on.

For years people have told Barbara she needed to write down her stories, but she was always reluctant, never wanting the focus to be on her. A very dynamic Christian lady, Elizabeth Newbold, who taught Bible studies in Birmingham in the early sixties, told Barbara that she was going to quit teaching the studies. Stunned, Barbara asked her why in the world she would do that. Elizabeth responded, "When the ladies talk more about Elizabeth than Christ, then there is something seriously wrong." Barbara lives by that same philosophy. She doesn't want anything to distract from Jesus.

In 2003, unfortunately, I found myself in an unemployed state and bored to death. As I asked the Lord what I should do while looking for a job, I felt His prompting me to write Barbara's stories down. My first response was, "Lord, You have to be kidding. I'm an accountant not a writer. This is a cruel joke." But in obedience alone, I checked out all 24 tapes from the Briarwood library and sat down to transcribe stories. Two weeks later I had 75 typed pages.

I took the typed stories to Barbara and told her she could do anything she wanted with them, but my suggestion was to give them to a "real" writer. She told me she thought I should be the one to continue because I knew her heart – that she didn't want to be the focus. That was the beginning of trusting God with each detail of this project. I can't tell you how many times I sat down at the computer completely frustrated and without a word to type. I would see one sentence to correct which led to another sentence and before I knew it several hours had passed and I had made progress.

Barbara Barker has spent more than forty years learning at the feet of the Lord and, as a result, pours what she learns into the lives of others. Several years ago Barbara began pondering the question, "If I only had ten minutes with another Christian, what would I say to them?" That question disciplined her to condense her major life lessons into ten, fifteen minute devotions, which she later taught to her eighth grade Sunday School class. In this book we share these lessons, illustrating the points with personal stories and poems Barbara wrote. For those of you that are counting, the ten lessons were expanded to thirteen in order to expound on what it means to have a radical faith, allowing God to take us into the impossible places where we have to rely totally on

Him. A final chapter was added for encouragement to be faithful to the finish.

The following verse has meant a lot to me throughout this process: *"Remember your leaders, who spoke the word of God to you. Consider the outcome of their way of life and imitate their faith"* *(Hebrews 13:7).*

May God use this book to build His truth into your life, conform you into His likeness, and overflow into the lives of others — all for His great glory. *"We have not stopped praying for you and asking God to fill you with the knowledge of His will through all spiritual wisdom and understanding. And we pray this in order that you may live a life worthy of the Lord and may please Him in every way, bearing fruit in every good work, growing in the knowledge of God, being strengthened with all power according to His glorious might so that you may have great endurance and patience, and joyfully giving thanks to the Father, who has qualified you to share in the inheritance of the saints in the kingdom of light"* *(Colossians 1:9-12).*

How to Use This Book

Our goal for this book is to provide a tool people use to grow in their walks with the Lord, so that they would be testimonies to the grace and goodness of God.

This book was patterned after Barbara's teaching style. Each chapter discusses an important Biblical life lesson illustrated with her personal stories and poems. So that you will have a frame of reference for her stories, I suggest that you read the preface which is an abbreviated version of Barbara's testimony. (The longer version is contained in Appendix 1.) The story illustrations throughout the book will make more sense once you understand her background.

At the end of each chapter there is a prayer, Bible study, and personal application and discussion questions. To maximize the impact of the lessons, I recommend you complete the personal application questions and Bible study. The Bible studies were written to expound on the chapters' lessons and facilitate application of the truths. The discussion questions may be helpful for those who desire to use the book in group Bible study settings.

Appendix 2 contains several humorous "Barbara stories," which have no spiritual merit, but are entertaining.

I pray that God will richly bless you through this book and use you mightily in the furtherance of His kingdom.

Denise Hamilton

PREFACE

How It All Began

(For a longer version see Appendix 1)

I (Barbara) grew up in Birmingham, Alabama, in a wonderful family with parents who served the Lord and taught me to respect God and be grateful for all that He did. But somehow I missed the truth of the Gospel and lived my life based on a works philosophy, which meant I believed that God's goodness to me was based on living a morally upright life. Since my one motivating desire was to excel in ballet, I tried to be a good person so God would bless me there. In my mind, my career was dependent on God's blessing and God's blessing was dependent on how good I could be. As a result I was a real "goody-goody" and, unrelated, He blessed my dancing. From age 11 and all the way through high school, I poured myself into this one pursuit, even dancing the lead for the local ballet company.

After high school, I was awarded a scholarship to a ballet school in Chicago where I attended Northwestern University and also performed with an ensemble. While home the summer after my freshman year, I received a letter from Frank, a young man I grew up with in Birmingham. He was a senior and a lifeguard at the country club when I was in seventh grade. As I sat by the pool, I listened to the older girls tell wild tales about him. He was what we called a "really bad boy." I remember thinking, "Good girls like me would never go out with wild boys like him." Yet the years passed and I would see him at parties and other events around town, watching him from a distance. I knew his name, but I didn't think he knew I existed. Frank had graduated from Auburn University and, this particular summer, he was in Pensacola, Florida attending Navy flight training. He was coming home for the weekend and had written asking me to go out with him. It was at that moment that I realized why good girls like me didn't go out with bad boys like him – they don't ask us. Because when he asked, I was really eager to go. I was surprised at how eager I was. Well, anyway, I said yes and we went out.

We fell in love that summer and decided to marry when I finished college. So for the "joy set before me" (marrying Frank), I finished the next three years of my college in two, which was remarkable given my dancing commitments. Right after graduation, I flew out to the West Coast to meet his aircraft carrier that was coming in from Korea. The Frank who got off the ship was very different from the Frank who had left eight months earlier. His foul language had improved and he was no longer drinking. He was much more serious and even talked a little about God. However, the biggest shock was that he no longer talked about marriage. His excuse was that he needed to get out of the Navy before even considering getting married. So I went to Houston, Texas where I was around a lot of exciting people. But the only thing that really excited me was seeing Frank during the few times we got together.

Eventually the time came for him to get out of the Navy and he planned to come to Houston immediately. By that time I was ready to give up everything to marry him. But I was in for a great shock. Frank said we still couldn't get married because he was going to seminary to become a preacher! Something was terribly wrong. The only explanation I could think of was that he had gotten really scared flying jets off aircraft carriers and had made some kind of crazy deal with God. If I could just be patient, he would eventually come to his senses. When he got to seminary, he would realize he had none of the qualities that would qualify him to be a preacher.

Knowing that Frank would quickly see going to seminary was a mistake, I went back to Birmingham to dance with the local theatre group and teach junior high school. Unfortunately, after six months in seminary, Frank told me that we were never going to get married. While in the Navy he had come to a sincere repentance toward God (sorry for all of his sinful behavior of the past) and decided the only way to balance the "bad" in his life was to go all the way in the other direction and be a preacher. In seminary he began digging into the Bible and realized that there was more to being a Christian than affirming the right things about God. He found that God offers man a supernatural, personal relationship with Him. Since Frank didn't have this kind of relationship with God, he determined to eliminate everything that would hinder him from devoting his life completely to the Lord. So he got rid of me.

At that point my world fell apart totally and completely. Even though I was still dancing, the career I had once dreamed of was no longer a possibility. My professional momentum was gone. I had invested my life in two things, dancing and Frank, and now they were both gone. I felt like I was in a really bad dream.

I immediately shook my fist in God's face. I had been so good; how could He have let this happen to me? Even in college when no one went to church, I got up and went. I might not have understood what was being said, but I was there. And even more difficult, I had kept a morally clean slate with that bad, bad boy. With my two most important things gone, life no longer had any meaning. I had nothing to live for, so I took a whole bottle of aspirin, cursed God, and lay down on my bed to die.

To my surprise, the next morning I woke up perfectly fine except for splotches all over my face. Mama came in and said, "Barbara, you have the measles!" She took me to the doctor, who confirmed her diagnosis. He sent me home to recuperate for a week in a darkened room. But deep down I knew it wasn't measles; obviously, **something** had intervened.

During that week, I lay in bed and thought about my life. I knew that God had supernaturally spared me, which was a very humbling realization. My older sister, Anita, who had been a Christian for a long time, would come and talk to me. She sat on my bed and told me she had prayed for years that I would come to the end of my self-sufficiency and see that I needed God. What did she mean by that? I had gone to church all my life. Then she actually implied that I was a sinner. Now that was a blow and I resented it. She obviously did not know what sin was. She hadn't been exposed to the things I had experienced in the dance world and among those "bad Navy pilots." I was pure in comparison. She obviously lived in a sheltered environment and didn't know what real sin was. But very lovingly she took me to the Scriptures where in I John 3:4b it says that *"sin is transgression of the Law"* and in Matthew 23:37-40 where God's Law is defined by Christ as *"loving God with all of our heart, mind, and strength and our neighbor as ourselves."* Maybe I measured up pretty well with the people I'd been around, but compared to God's standard I fell terribly short.

In one afternoon I went from the height of self-righteousness to the depth of being a sinner headed for eternal separation from God. As moral and "churchy" as I thought I was, the truth was that I was a sinner. In God's eyes all my righteousness was as "filthy rags." Never before understanding the concept of judgment or hell, its reality was very clear in the Scriptures and, at that point, it was my destination. Then Anita left my room.

She came back the next day and told me that God loved me unconditionally and provided forgiveness for my sins through His Son Jesus Christ. She said that for me to be reconciled to God, I needed to put my trust and hope of salvation in the sacrificial death of Jesus. All I had to do was acknowledge what He did for me on the cross, receive Him as my Savior, and commit my life to Him. After that long night of looking death and hell squarely in the face, that was the best news I could ever hear. I wanted the gift so badly, but I was terrified of the cost. I wasn't sure if I was ready to trust God completely with my life. What if He wanted me to go to Africa? I would have to think about such a surrender a little bit more.

The next morning the truth of Romans 8:32 came to me. Even though I didn't know the verse at the time, its logic was clear. It says, *"He who did not spare his own Son, but gave him up for us all—how will he not also, along with him, graciously give us all things?"* Doesn't it make sense that if He freely gave His own Son, paying the ultimate cost, He would surely meet all my other needs? With that thought I got down on my knees and asked Him to come into my life, surrendering all I knew of myself into His open arms. My heart was still shattered into a million pieces and my future an uncertain maze, but I had a confidence and assurance that I had Jesus. And He was enough. Everything else was going to be okay.

After my miraculous recovery from "the measles," I went anywhere and everywhere Christians were studying the Bible or praying. I lived vicariously through others' experiences of trusting God, leaning on them to tell me what the Bible said and pray for me. But God saved me for something much better than that.

God soon led me out of the security of the Bible Belt to the West Coast where I lived and worked among people that had no idea what it meant to be a follower of Christ. Spiritually cutoff from other believers and not knowing how to pray or study the Bible for myself, I felt very out touch with God.

In desperation, one night I fell on my knees and prayed, "God, you have to help me. I can't do it alone." Suddenly I felt as if He was standing right behind me saying, *"Come to me, all you who are weary and burdened, and I will give you rest" (Matthew 11:28),* and was incredibly aware of God's availability through prayer. Also, about that time I came to know that He had already sent me a teacher, the Holy Spirit. Additionally, *What the Bible is All About* by Henrietta Meers, which condenses the truths of the Bible, book by book, helped me tremendously. Over the next several years, I grew spiritually and learned that His love and my fellowship with Him were not dependent on other people.

During that time, my zeal for the Lord grew so greatly that I decided to move back to Birmingham and apply for Bible college. One day as I was filling out an application, my mother came to my room and told me I had a telephone call. Time seemed to slow down and my heart stopped beating. Somehow I knew who it was. I answered the phone and sure enough it was that "bad" Navy pilot who had broken up with me four years earlier to attend seminary and work his way to heaven. Through an Air Force chaplain, Frank had come to understand that what he was working so hard to do, Christ had already accomplished for him. Frank had put his trust in Jesus' finished work on the cross as his hope of salvation. That summer he had come to Birmingham to start a Presbyterian church in a storefront on the outskirts of the city. Hearing that I was back in town, he called to see if I would have coffee with him.

That was one of the most exciting nights of my life. We talked and talked, trying to catch each other up on the past four years. At 12:15 a.m., he reached over and grabbed my hand. I thought the butterflies in my stomach would fly out my ears. He said, "Barbara, why do you think that God has saved us for each other and brought us both back to Birmingham?"

I wanted to shout, "I don't know, but marry me tonight before you change your mind again." Instead, what came out of my mouth was, "I don't know, but until I know what God wants to do, I won't go one step further." My response was a miracle. I realized then that God had worked very deeply in my life in that I wasn't willing to compromise my relationship with Him, even for a relationship with Frank.

Over the weeks that followed, we prayed and waited and eventually became convinced that God indeed had brought us together for His purpose. In our little storefront church, I became Mrs. Frank M. Barker, Jr. on November 3, 1961.

We were an hour out of town before I realized I had a note my sister slipped into my hand when we left. I opened the note and saw she had written Matthew 6:33, *"But seek first his kingdom and his righteousness, and all these things will be given to you as well."* We pulled off the highway right then and asked God to let that be the story of our lives.

That was a glorious beginning and it lasted a week.

After waiting for Frank for eight years, I was so excited to finally be his wife. I thought he would meet all of my needs. He would make me happy, make me feel secure, and adore me. But he didn't do any of those things. My disappointment was crushing. To add to my insecurity, we had three babies in two-and-a-half years and up to that point I had never babysat, nor changed a diaper.

Frank was working hard to grow and pastor this new church and it seemed like everything was more important to him than me. I tried very hard to find my place. But all I was qualified to do was dance and there wasn't much of a demand for a dancing preacher's wife. My life had been spent on stage, needing the applause it brought, and now there was nothing I could do.

Even Frank admits that he was wrong in how he compromised his responsibilities as a husband and father during those early years of our marriage. But his heart was always so bent toward the Lord, that had God shown him his mistakes, I am certain Frank would have changed. I know now that God purposely kept Frank's eyes closed to my needs until He did the necessary work in me. However, by not looking for God's master plan, I became bitter, angry, and played the pitiful martyr. I would put on my "preacher's wife face" and say to the people at church, "God bless you. Praise the Lord." My drama training finally came in handy. But while I put up a good front for the outside world, Frank and the children knew the real me.

In that miserable state, I lost all ability to pray and read my Bible. Consumed with anger and bitterness, I lost all assurance of my salvation and I wanted to take my life.

One day in my desperation I fell down on my face on the den floor. My three babies, Anita at 2½ years old, Frank III at 1½, and Peggy at six months, were somewhere in the house. Looking back, I don't know where they were; an angel must have been babysitting. I cried out to God, "I can't take it anymore. I can't talk to You. I can't live with You. But I can't live without You. I'm miserable. You have to send me some help."

God heard my prayer and showed me two things that afternoon. First, *"My people have committed two sins: they have forsaken me, the spring of living water, and have dug their own cisterns, broken cisterns that cannot hold water" (Jeremiah 2:13)*. You have forsaken Me, the Fountain of living water and yet wonder why you're dying of thirst. When you had nothing, you found your total sufficiency in Me. But when I gave you Frank, you transferred all of your expectations to him. He was never designed to meet the need in your life that only I can. Come back to Me and let Me fill your life. Let your expectations be of Me." Deep down inside I understood what He was trying to show me.

Secondly, I imagined Adam in the Garden of Eden. God had told him to till the Garden and that was what Adam was doing. Then God said, *"It's not good for the man to be alone" (Genesis 2:18).* So He sent him a helper to assist him in that which he was called to do. But Eve led him to the tree of forbidden fruit. It was like God said, "I brought Frank here to cultivate this part of My vineyard and I gave you to him to help him. But you are distracting him and pulling him away." My marriage was fighting against the ministry. God showed me that day marriage was my ministry and I was to walk worthy of that calling, with all lowliness and meekness.

I broke under the loving, gentle hand of God and hours went by where I just communed with God. Rising from the floor, I felt a new resurrection inside. Fortunately, about the same time, God began to open Frank's eyes to my needs and his legitimate responsibilities as my husband. I believe this marked the real beginning of our Christian marriage. From that point on, it was two steps forward and one step back, but at least we were headed in the right direction. I am so glad that God kept him blinded until I personally learned those very hard lessons.

Over the past forty plus years since, I have sought to know God more and make Him known to others. Many times the spiritual lessons were learned the hard way, with much pain. What I would give to prevent you from repeating my same mistakes! If I could sit down with each of you for just a few minutes, I would love to pass on what I have learned. The following chapters were written with that desire in mind.

CHAPTER 1

God's Word is True

The first great foundational truth that every believer needs to know is "God's Word is true." Establishing a foundation on the fact that the Bible is **the** source of all truth seems obvious. But today more than ever before, this fact is being challenged throughout the Church. Christians are being conformed to the world's way of living, guided by feelings and desires instead of the truths of Scripture. They have come to accept the world's message that there are no absolute rights or wrongs.

Everyone lives by one of two authority systems: either the reason of man or the revelation of God. An authority system is how one determines what is true, wise, and good. For some, their source of truth is based on their, or someone else's, personal opinion, teaching, or belief – the reason of man. How many times do you hear someone say, "I think . . .," "It seems to me . . .," "Authorities report . . .," "I read somewhere . . .," or "Polls show . . ."? If we really think about it, whose opinion is **not** based on his or her own perspective or experience? But there is such insecurity in this. In what or whom can we really trust? Can we trust newspapers, TV, politicians, preachers, friends, or relatives? To whom can we go and know that 100% of the time, without a shadow of a doubt, we will be told the truth? The answer is no one, not even our selves.

Everyone lives by one of two authority systems, either the reason of man or the revelation of God.

The seat of authority in life must not be one's own reasoning, or anyone else's. Instead it should be God's truth as it is revealed in Scripture. Some would doubt its ability to be the source of truth by saying that the Bible is just a book written by men. Although men penned the words, each word they wrote was inspired by God (2 Timothy 3:16a and II Peter 1:21). The Bible that we have today was written by approximately 40 men from many different walks of life over a period of 1500 years. Each one's teaching is consistent with all the others. That in and of itself is truly miraculous. When have you ever heard of that many people agreeing on the same message?

The Bible contains information that could have only come from God. In the Old Testament alone there are over 2,000 prophecies, none of which have ever been proven false. Approximately 300 of those were fulfilled in the events covered by the writings of the New Testament. Hundreds of them point in intricate detail toward the life and work of Jesus Christ. Most were fulfilled in His first coming and the rest will happen when He comes again.

Christ, His life, death, and resurrection, is the scarlet thread message that runs throughout the entire Bible. What is the likelihood that one man could live a life that met the conditions of all of the Biblical prophecies combined? Old Testament prophets gave the location of His birth, His ancestral lineage, and details of his life, betrayal, death, and resurrection. Eight hundred years before the use of the cross for executions, Scripture predicted the Messiah's death on the cross. In his book, *Science Speaks*, Dr. Peter Stoner calculates the chances of only eight of the hundreds of these specific prophecies being fulfilled in one man at one point of time as being the same as covering the state of Texas two feet deep in silver dollars, marking one with an "X," and expecting a blind man to pick it out on his first try. For you mathematicians, that likelihood is one in ten to the 17th power (10 followed by 17 zeros)! [1]

Christ, the incarnate God, quoted often from Scripture. In the book of Matthew alone, Jesus quoted from what we now refer to as the Old Testament approximately 30 times. His life was a fulfillment of Scripture and not once did He stray from its teachings.

The Scriptures have been subjected to God's special care. No other ancient document exists with such authenticity. Men and women throughout the centuries have sacrificed their lives to ensure that it remains intact and accurate. Additionally, as man advances in scientific and archeological knowledge, each new discovery only authenticates the Scriptures, rather than discrediting them. Man knows of nothing today that can contradict God's Word.

(Note: I have just scratched the surface on this topic. There are many excellent books which you should read to understand the subject more thoroughly, including *Evidence that Demands a Verdict* by Josh McDowell and *The Case for Christ* by Lee Strobel.)

But most importantly, there is the evidence of the Bible's life-changing power as we look around us. Each Christian is a living testimony to its effectiveness. We can give all kinds of intellectual arguments as to the Bible's authority, but there is no greater evidence than seeing someone whose life was changed because he or she met Jesus personally and understood the truths of Scripture.

Scripture tells us that the Word of God *"is living and active and sharper than any double- edged sword" (Hebrews 4:12)*. This document has transforming power. In Psalm 119 we learn that by internalizing and living out the Word we are blessed (v. 1), strengthened (v. 28), kept pure (v. 9), and comforted (v. 52). The Word gives us more insight than our teachers (v. 99) and makes us wiser than our enemies (v. 98). It is a lamp unto our feet and light on our path (v. 105) and causes us to hate the wrong paths (v. 128).

I am no scientist and have little knowledge of the teachings of evolutionary biology, but I cannot fathom how someone closes his eyes to the truth of Scripture. If the theory of evolution is accurate, how could a male and a female, who are both needed for the reproduction of offspring, evolve at exactly the same rate with compatible and inter-dependent anatomies? And this would have to be true in every species. Also, how could fish gills evolve into lungs without the fish's drowning? Why do we not see evolving creatures today? Why are there no missing links in the fossil record? Where is the origin of humans' personality, abstract thinking, and language? And most confusing of all — why do intelligent people ignore such glaring weaknesses in their belief system?

The reason men and women do not believe is simple. If we believe in the act of creation, we have to acknowledge a Creator. And if there is a Creator, He must have a plan and that plan must involve us. It only makes sense that the One who created the world knows what life is all about and that the One who **is** Truth would tell us what is really true. The Author of Life tells us where we came from and the One who passed through death and sits on the other side can tell us what happens when we die. The One who created us knows what is best for us. Therefore, the logical conclusion is that this Holy Creator God, Who sets the rules for what is right and wrong, also establishes the consequences for the breaking of His laws.

Everything Christians believe is written in this amazing document. We believe that *"all Scripture is God-breathed and is useful for **teaching**, for **rebuking**, for **correction**, for **training in righteousness**, so that the man of God may be thoroughly equipped for every good work" (II Timothy 3:16-17, emphasis added)*. The Bible is the source of all truth and should be the foundation of our **teaching**. We don't just make up what we believe.

As we read the Truth, God shows us areas in which we differ from Him. **Rebuking** is God's warning that we are on the wrong path, whether intentionally or unintentionally. The Bible tells us where we veered off into the wrong direction.

For twenty-two years I thought of myself as a good little girl, after all that's what my mama told me. And I was certainly better than that "bad Navy pilot" and all those "immoral people" with whom I worked. When my sister took me to the Word of God, I realized that I didn't love Him as I should. I realized that sin wasn't what I did, but what I was. This was the truth that brought me to repentance toward God and ultimately to salvation. But that was only the beginning. Up to that point in my life, **I** was the center of my world. Through Scripture I came to know that life was not about me. God created me to live for Him.

If **rebuking** is the stop sign that tells us "the bridge ahead is out," then **correction** is the sign that points us to the appropriate route leading to our destination. Once on the right path, **training in righteousness** will show us how to continue to live a life pleasing to God.

Someone once said, "This Book contains the mind of God, the state of man, the way of salvation, the doom of sinners, and the happiness of believers. Its doctrines are holy, its precepts are binding, its histories are true, and its decisions are immutable. Read it to be wise, believe it to be safe, and practice it to be holy."

Joshua 1:8 outlines the way to success: *"Do not let the Book of the Law depart from your mouth; meditate on it day and night, so that you may be careful to do everything written in it. Then you will be prosperous and successful."* Life can only be lived successfully in subjection to God's Word.

MY PRAYER

Dear Lord, many times I find it difficult to live in a world that does not think there is absolute truth, your Truth. Please help me to stand firmly rooted in Your teachings and be salt and light to those around me. I know that I have to rely on your strength and your wisdom to do this. Thank you for your promise of provision in these areas. Amen.

Notes

[1] Stoner, Peter W., *Science Speaks*, (Chicago, Illinois: Moody Press, © 1958, 1963, 1968, http://www.geocities.com/stoner don/science_speaks.html, accessed 12-21-06).

Chapter 1
PERSONAL APPLICATION

1. Ask God to search your heart, thoughts, motives, and actions. In what ways have you conformed to the world's teachings and not followed God?

2. When was the last time God convicted you through His Word?

3. Think of specific ways that you can develop more discipline to transform your mind using God's Word.

Chapter 1
BIBLE STUDY

What does the Bible say about itself?

- Jeremiah 36:2

- II Timothy 3:16-17

- Hebrews 4:12

- II Peter 1:20-21

- Revelation 22:18-19

No other document in human history is more authentic than the Bible and none other has come under such attack from people intent on it eradication. Why has the Bible survived intact? See Isaiah 40:8 and Matthew 5:18.

The Bible's internal evidence of its own authenticity:

There has never been a prophecy in the Bible proven to be untrue. More than 200 prophecies alone were fulfilled in the first coming of Christ. Match the following Old Testament prophecies to its New Testament fulfillment.

Old Testament prophecies:
   Psalm 22:18
   Isaiah 53:12

Zechariah 9:9
Zechariah 12:10
Isaiah 53:9
Psalm 16:10
Isaiah 7:14
Psalm 34:20
Micah 5:2
Psalm 22:16
Zechariah 11:12
Jeremiah 23:5

New Testament fulfillments:

Jesus would be born of a virgin. (Matthew 1:18-25):

He would be of the house of David. (Luke 3:31):

He would be born in Bethlehem. (Matthew 2:1):

He would enter Jerusalem on a donkey. (Luke 19:35-37):

He would be betrayed for 30 pieces of silver. (Matthew 26:15):

His hands and feet would be pierced. (Luke 32:33; John 20:25):

He would be crucified with thieves (Mt. 27:38):

Lots would be cast for His garments. (John 19:24):

His bones would not be broken. (John 19:33):

His side would be pierced. (John 19:34):

He would be buried with the rich. (Matthew 27:57-60):

He would be resurrected. (Acts 2:31):

What does the Bible say about prophecies?

- Deuteronomy 18:22

- Isaiah 46:9-11

- II Peter 1:20-21

Jesus gave authenticity to the Old Testament when He quoted from it (Luke 24:27). Give the Old Testament references for the following quotes of Jesus. (Note: These are just a few of many.)

- Matthew 4:4

- Matthew 4:7

- Matthew 4:10

What was the circumstance in which Jesus quoted these verses? Do you see any application to your life today?

Many would discount the miracles of the Bible as allegorical stories at best. What would Jesus say about that (Matthew 12:38-41)?

What are some results of knowing and applying God's Word?
- Psalm 119:11
- Psalm 119:28
- Psalm 119:45
- Psalm 119:46
- Psalm 119:52
- Psalm 119:98-99
- Psalm 119:104a
- Psalm 119:105
- Psalm 119:128
- Psalm 119:165

What are our responsibilities as to God's Word?
- Psalm 119:1-2
- Psalm 119:7
- Psalm 119:11
- Psalm 119:15
- Psalm 119:16
- Psalm 119:43
- Psalm 119:46
- Psalm 119:62
- Colossians 3:16

Chapter 1
DISCUSSION QUESTIONS

1. Under which authority system do you live – the reason of man or the revelation of God? How is that evidenced in your life?

2. List specific instances of how God has used your study of the Bible to transform your life?
   - Teaching

   - Rebuking

   - Correction

   - Training in righteousness

3. How would you respond to someone who said there is no "absolute truth"?

4. How has belief in evolution, which contradicts the Bible's teaching of the earth's origin, weakened the foundation of our society? Think hard.

CHAPTER 2

Obedience is the Evidence of Belief

What you say is what you know.
What you do is what you believe.
(Unknown)

Many times the way we live contradicts what we say we believe. We ignore the reproof of Scripture and follow another "authority system" which seems to be logical, good, right, and desirable. The Bible tells us that *"there is a way that seems right to a man, but in the end it leads to death" (Proverbs 14:12).*

When I married, someone gave me a little Sunbeam hand mixer. Since I did not know how to cook, I never used it. Right before our first child, Anita, was born, I tried to paint a chest but the paint would not mix. So I thought about that egg beater. Sure enough, it made the paint as smooth as silk. I couldn't believe how creative I was. After the chest was painted, I cleaned the beaters with turpentine and put the mixer back in its box on the shelf. A few months later, I needed to whip cream and reached for my little egg beater. Immediately after turning it on, sparks flew and smoke billowed out of the plug. Without my realizing it, little drops of paint had gotten into the motor and ruined it. That incident helped me understand Proverbs 14:12 cited in the previous paragraph. The mixer came with an instruction book that told me what it was to be used for and how to take care of it, which I totally ignored. I took what was clearly made for one purpose and used it in a way which "seemed right" and served my immediate need. Isn't that what we do with our lives? Why are we seeing the disintegration of our society as well as the Church? We have ignored the truths given to us by our Creator. We no longer see the Bible as "our instruction book;" instead, we follow our own fallible reason to "destruction."

Several years ago a young lady who was divorcing her husband came to talk with Frank. When he asked her the reason for the divorce, she told him that she wasn't happy in her marriage. His response was, "God is more interested in your holiness than your happiness." Frank guided her through Scripture that showed God's view of the sacredness of marriage and the importance of their staying together. Unfortunately, she ignored everything the Bible said and went through with the divorce. Why did the Bible not enter into her decision-making process? Because she wanted her way more than she wanted God's way, she ignored its clear teaching.

Do **you** truly believe the Bible or are you just giving lip service to your belief? When your desires and Scripture collide, which one wins? What is the evidence in your life that you believe the Word is true? The evidence should be that the Bible becomes the rule of authority in your life, determining your decisions and marking your course.

There is a critical difference between an intellectual assent to God's Word and actually doing God's will as outlined in Scripture. True faith will be verified by the life that we live and demonstrated by our actions. *"Faith by itself, if it is not accompanied by action, is dead" (James 2:17).* To say one has faith is pointless unless there are actions to prove it. Demons even believe in the existence of God, but they do not possess saving faith. *"The man who says, 'I know him,' but does not do what he commands is a liar, and the truth is not in him. But if anyone obeys his word, God's love is truly made complete in him. This is how we know we are in him: Whoever claims to live in him must walk as Jesus did" (I John 2:4-6).*

When Anita was a little girl, I asked her to pick up her toys. After a few minutes she came in the house with a handful of caladium leaves. Those particular plants were my pride and joy because it wasn't often that I had a successful gardening experience. She had gone out and picked the colorful leaves that I had planted and carefully nurtured. Seeing them in her hand, I knew the pretty plants were over for that year. She presented them to me saying, "I love you, Mama." All I could think was that my garden was ruined and her toys were still not picked up. Suddenly I realized I often express my love for God in the same way Anita did. I try to redefine love in a way that is more convenient and comfortable for me, rather than how God requires love to be expressed. *"Whoever has my commands and obeys them, he is the one who loves me. He who loves me will be loved by my Father, and I too will love him and show myself to him" (John 14:21).* It is important to obey God on His terms and not on our own. Do we ignore clear commands of Scripture and then try to please God with "spiritual behavior"? Do we think that praising God and telling Him that we love Him can compensate for blatant disobedience?

> ### *Do we ignore the clear commands of Scripture and then try to please God with "spiritual behavior"?*

How then do we begin to internalize the Bible so that our actions demonstrate our faith? First, we must commit to a regular and consistent study of the Scriptures. Although this may be the toughest battle in a Christian's life, time should be set aside every day to read and study. In addition, getting into a Bible study with other believers will hold you accountable to dig into the Scriptures for yourself.

Much Biblical truth can be gleaned from Scripture-based sermons, if we listen carefully. Desiring to teach our children to pay attention in church, we taught them to take notes on what they heard. This tradition started when they were six, old enough to stay in big church. I regret to tell you that we paid them to do it, but we did. They received a quarter when they turned in good notes. Over lunch we asked them to tell us one thing they learned, which was a good springboard into discussing how to apply spiritual truths. There is such a tendency to listen to something and then let it fade away the next day, not giving the lesson an opportunity to affect us.

Memorizing and meditating on Biblical passages are essential to the internalizing of Scriptures. There are many techniques and methods of doing this. I find it helpful to choose longer passages, rather than single verses. I read them, think about them, paraphrase them, ask God how to apply them in my own life, and then read them over and over again until I no longer need to refer to the written passage.

Lastly, the very best way to learn Scripture is to teach it. *"Let the word of Christ dwell in you richly as you teach and admonish one another with all wisdom . . ." (Colossians 3:16).* As you overflow your lessons into the lives of other people, the truths will become more of a part of you. Ask God to give you an opportunity to share what you learn and He will answer that prayer. If you are intimidated, start by teaching something small like a children's Sunday School class or a backyard Bible club. Just step out in faith, trusting the Lord to teach through you. Remember the Holy Spirit, Who lives inside of you, will be your teacher as well as theirs.

One of the primary reasons the world is not impacted by the Church of our day is that the people who profess to believe in God do not demonstrate the truths they espouse. How can our whole society be so morally bankrupt when polls show that a large percentage of adults profess to be born again Christians? Why is the divorce rate in the Church no better than it is among those who do not profess faith in Christ? Movies and television programs flaunting the very things God hates are accepted and enjoyed by Christians as well as those who have no concern for what God approves. "Born again" Christians visit pornographic websites in astonishing numbers. Activities in the business community reveal that even Christians are often willing to overlook personal integrity for "the bottom line." Retail stores and shopping malls flourish on Sundays although Christians have been clearly forbidden by God to conduct "business as usual" on that day. Materialism and the pursuit of self-indulgent pleasures preoccupy believers in the same way as it does for those outside the Church.

If the values, goals, and desires of Christians do not reflect concern for the Will of God as revealed in the Word of God, why should the world be impressed with the Message Christians bring?

MY PRAYER

Father, I confess that many times I have taken Your precious Word for granted. Please forgive me and help me to love it as life itself. Help me to make it a priority in my life – to study it, memorize it, meditate it, and teach it. Teach me its great truths and then help me live out those truths daily. Give me opportunities to overflow them into others. I join Jeremiah

(15:16) in saying, *"When Your words came, I ate them; they were my joy and my heart's delight; for I hear Your name, O Lord God Almighty."* Amen.

Chapter 2
PERSONAL APPLICATION

1. Do you read and study Scripture daily? If not, what is your plan to begin doing so? Who can hold you accountable?

2. What has been the most effective method for you to memorize Scripture? What can you do to improve your Scripture memorization?

3. Give specific ways that you can overflow what you are learning in your personal Bible study into others.

4. Is there in an area in your life in which you are ignoring a clear command of Scripture?

Chapter 2
BIBLE STUDY

Ezra was a Jewish priest and teacher of the Scriptures who returned to Jerusalem from Babylonian Captivity in 458 B.C. How does the Bible describe him?

- Ezra 7:6

- Ezra 7:10

- Ezra 7:25

Following Ezra's example, how should we handle God's Word?

Paraphrase II Timothy 2:15.

How does one "correctly handle the Word of Truth"?

Read Luke 6:46-49. What is the connection between hearing the Word and doing the Word?

What are the results of hearing and doing versus hearing and ignoring? Why?

Read Ephesians 2:8-9 and James 2:17. Do these passages contradict each other? Why or why not?

Read I John 2:4-6. How is God's love made complete through obedience?

Obedience to God's Word expresses our thankfulness to Him for what He has done for us. It shines a spotlight on Him and sets us apart from those whose eyes are darkened to the truth. We have to depend on Him to live "rightly" because obedience that pleases God is impossible without Him.

What does God promise for those who obey?
- Deuteronomy 5:29

- Joshua 1:8

- James 1:25

Chapter 2
DISCUSSION QUESTIONS

1. Why is spiritual behavior without one's heart being right so offensive to God?

2. What tools have been helpful to you in your study of Scripture?

3. What is the difference between preparing a lesson to teach someone and sitting at the Master's feet and learning a lesson to share with others? Which is the most effective?

4. What are specific steps you can take to ensure that your children regularly study the Bible on their own?

CHAPTER 3

The Way "Up" Is "Down"

One of the greatest paradoxes of the Christian life is that the teachings of Scripture are in dramatic contradiction to what the world around us teaches. As Christians we are commanded to emulate Christ's character qualities of **humility, sacrifice, giving,** and **servanthood.** In contrast, the world is telling us to "assert yourself;" "protect, maintain, demand your rights;" "rise up and rule over others;" "look out for number one;" "get to the top;" "be served;" "grab all the gusto you can;" etc. How upside down God's Kingdom is compared to the world! Truth is:

- We must humble ourselves to be exalted,
- Die to live,
- Give to receive, and
- The servant is greater than the master.

HUMILITY PRECEDES HONOR

As Christians we should be committed to living a lifestyle that is totally different from the rest of the world. When the world says, "Look out for number one," the Bible tells us to die to ourselves and put God and others first. A fact often ignored in our modern day Christianity is that we live in a God-centered universe, not a man-centered one. God's glory is the central issue of life, not one's importance, feelings, comfort, happiness, etc. We have to remember that God is the Creator, King, Sustainer, Judge, and Redeemer. His Being is all-glorious. He is perfect truth, holiness, justice, love, wisdom, mercy, power, and totally sovereign over all creation. He is complete in Himself and in need of nothing. He is the One we are to serve, not ourselves. When He was here on earth, Jesus demonstrated how this is to be done.

One of the most amazing truths in all of creation is that Jesus Christ, the Second Person of the Trinity, *"Though he was God, did not demand and cling to his rights as God, but laid aside his mighty power and glory, taking the disguise of a slave and becoming like men. And he humbled himself even further, going so far as actually to die a criminal's death on a cross" (Philippians 2:6-8 – Living).* And the reason He did this was to redeem (pay the penalty for the sin of) fallen man, whom He loved, and to restore him to the relationship with God for which he was created. God's admonition to us is: *"Your attitude should be the same as Christ Jesus" (Philippians 2:5).*

Someone has said of Frank:
"It is not that he thinks lowly of himself,
it is just that
he does not think of himself at all."

When most people describe Frank they use the word "humble." It is not that he thinks lowly of himself; it is just that he does not think of himself at all. His humility is not a sign of weakness; you will never find a stronger man as a defender of the faith. So what does it mean to be humble? Andrew Murray in his book, *Humility*, defined it as: "the sense of entire nothingness, which comes when we see how truly God is all, and in which we make way for God to be all." [1] Murray goes on to say, "Humility is not so much a grace or virtue along with others; it is the root of all, because it alone takes the right attitude before God, and allows Him as God to do all." [2]

Jesus said in Matthew 18:4, *"Therefore, whoever humbles himself like this child is the greatest in the kingdom of heaven."* Micah 6:8 instructs, *"He has showed you, O man, what is good. And what does the LORD require of you? To act justly and to love mercy and to walk humbly with your God."* Other good verses are: *"Humble yourselves before the Lord, and he shall lift you up" (James 4:10). "God opposes the proud but gives grace to the humble. Humble yourselves, therefore, under God's mighty hand, that he may lift you up in due time" (I Peter 5:5b-6).*

All of these verses instruct us to humble ourselves. So how do we go about it? We must recognize that pride and self-absorption, which are natural to each of us, are the opposite of humility. Dying to our own wants and desires is where humility begins. Read Philippians 2:3-11 and see Christ's example of humility. His focus was not on Himself; even though He was God, He looked out for the interests of others.

He made Himself nothing and was obedient to the Father, even to the point of physical death.

DEATH TO SELF PRECEDES LIFE

In the beginning days of our ministry, I learned a very valuable lesson on dying to self. Because I worked with the young people at the church, they seemed to camp out at our house. The constant demands of ministry were getting to me. I told Frank that I couldn't take anymore and I just had to have some alone time with him. He said that night, after we put the children to bed, we would turn out all the lights, get in our pajamas, and play Chinese Checkers in bed. We did just that, closed our bedroom door, and started playing checkers on the bed. Yes, we really were playing.

Suddenly I heard the back door open and someone say, "Barbara, Barbara, where are you?" The door stayed unlocked because a young man who lived with us never had his key. Then our bedroom door opened and a young couple just waltzed right in. I was horrified. They didn't say, "Oh, you're in the bed," "I'm sorry," or anything like that. They had a dating problem and wanted to talk to us about it. Modest as I am, I had the covers pulled up to my chin, but Frank sat there in his pajamas and talked to them like they were in his office.

After a while they left and I was turning to Frank to say I couldn't believe it, when the door opened again and two college girls appeared. One said, "Barbara, Mel and Cathy said you were still up. I want you to meet my new roommate at Samford."

Again, there was no apology or any indication of the inappropriateness of their behavior. Now, I am sure these kids were raised to know better, so God must have put blinders on their eyes in order for me to learn a lesson. The girls finally left and I burst into tears. "I can't stand it any longer. I have to have some privacy."

When women get emotional, men get very nervous. Frank said, "Barbara, calm down. Get a hold of yourself." I went on ranting for a little while longer before he stopped me and said, "What does Romans 12:1 say?"

I said, "I know what it says and it doesn't have anything to do with my bedroom."

Curtly he said, "Say it, Barbara. Say it."

Quickly, slurring the words together I said, *"Therefore, I urge you, brothers, in view of God's mercy, to offer your bodies as living sacrifices, holy and pleasing to God – this is your spiritual act of worship."*

He made me repeat it slower. Then he asked, "Present your bodies a what?"

"A living sacrifice," I said begrudgingly.

"Barbara, what is a living sacrifice?" I'll never forget the picture as long as I live. There he was in his blue pajamas with his arms outstretched, saying, "A living sacrifice is Jesus on the cross saying, 'Come unto me. I have no boundaries. I am always here with my arms held out.'" Right at that moment I didn't like the idea, so I rebelled, turned over, and tried to go to sleep. Eventually God worked that truth in my heart and I did repent. But I also started locking my bedroom door.

Real life and real fruitfulness only come after death, the death of our selves. Jesus says in John 12:24, *"I tell you the truth, unless a kernel of wheat falls to the ground and dies, it remains only a single seed. But if it dies, it produces many seeds."* Unfortunately, the dying process required for Christ-likeness is not a one time occurrence. Romans 12:1 tells us to present ourselves as a "living sacrifice." It has been said that the problem with a living sacrifice is that it keeps crawling off the altar. Dying to self must be a continual process done every day, moment by moment.

I was speaking to ministers' wives at Southeastern Bible College one Friday morning and said the following:

> "I have friends who are wives of military men. Those men can be gone for months at a time serving our country. Their wives understand that they and their husbands are called to a higher purpose. Life isn't about making sure they are cozy, comfortable, and happy. Their personal sacrifice is necessary so the rest of the people in our country can live safely and securely. Just like those wives, our husbands are called to battle, a spiritual battle. We must not view ministry as what we do only when it's convenient and fun. Ministry has its price. A huge sacrifice for us is time with our husbands. I had to train my children that

they might not get to see their daddy as much as some other children do. But they should be very grateful because he has been given a high calling from God."

As I spoke the words, I could sense the admiration of those young wives and my heart swelled with pride . . . but pride cometh before the fall.

Frank was out of town and due back on Sunday evening following my talk to the Bible College wives. I had arranged for someone to drive the children and me to church so we could ride back with him, thinking maybe we would get ice cream on the way home. He'd been gone for a week, so I knew he would be anxious to see his family. But at church he told me he had to talk with a man right afterwards and would be home as soon as he could. With a bite I told him, "We don't have a ride home. I assumed that you would want to see your family since you've been gone for a week."

He gave us a ride home and said as he was leaving, "Honey, I really hate not being able to help you get the children to bed, but this is a desperate situation and I really have to go."

I looked at him and snarled, "You don't have to worry about it. We don't need you. We get along without you just fine. Go see that man and take care of your church." Just as the words left my mouth I had a vision of all of those wide-eyed girls at Southeastern Bible College two days before thinking I was "such a Godly woman." What would they have thought of me right at that moment?

God continues to test my commitment to be a **living** sacrifice. And each time the dying to my own selfish ambitions and desires is painful. To not get discouraged, I have to remember that *"the one who calls you is faithful and he will do it"* (*I Thessalonians 5:24*). Dying to self is a necessary part of the sanctification process and God promised that He will perfect that which He began in me.

GIVING PRECEDES RECEIVING

How many books are available on how to get rich? Obviously, too many to count. It seems that everyone is pursuing the American dream of amassing wealth. Don't they know that they cannot take it with them? Jesus said, *"Do not store up for yourselves treasures on earth, where moth and rust destroy, and where thieves break in and steal. But store up for yourselves treasures in heaven, where moth and rust do not destroy, and where thieves do not break in and steal. For where your treasure is, there your heart will be also"* (*Matthew 6:19-21*).

Soon after he became a Christian, my husband, Frank, began investing a large portion of his income in the Kingdom. After we married, he continued that practice. But I did not like the idea. I could not see how even our basic needs would be met. I was raised in an affluent home, where every need and most wants were generously, but wisely, provided. As a result, I did not understand how to trust God to supply the every day necessities. Frank wanted us to learn to trust God totally and completely in every area of our lives, and the best way to learn, he thought, was by trusting Him with our finances. Relying on God to meet our needs, he gave just about everything we got away!

Now God doesn't lead everybody to live like that, but Frank thought if we were going to teach about the reality of faith, we had to personally experience trusting God in that way. So he led us on this wild adventure which has turned into the most exciting life I could ever imagine. We didn't let anyone know our needs except God. As a result, we watched Him provide in time and on time in more ways than I can recount. God has never failed us. And even more importantly, all three of our children, having experienced God's faithfulness firsthand, are now embracing the same life of faith.

I remember one month when we had several unanticipated bills, from the doctor to a broken septic tank, and it looked like we would be $700 short if God didn't supernaturally intervene. Our commitment was always that the bills would be paid on time, because if we gave money away while we had outstanding debts, we would be giving money that belonged to someone else. Although our policy was not to go into debt, right then it looked like there was no other option. On Sunday, I told Frank that the checks needed to be mailed by Thursday to meet the deadlines. With his simplistic faith, he told me that God would provide. We started praying.

Monday the mail came and there was nothing. Tuesday nothing. On Wednesday morning I asked God for some sign of encouragement that He was going to provide. Any little thing would do. In my quiet time that morning I happened to read, *"Are not five sparrows sold for two pennies? Yet not one of them is forgotten by God. Indeed, the very hairs of your head are all numbered. Don't be afraid; you are worth more than many sparrows" (Luke 12:6-7).* In the afternoon I went to the mailbox and there in the mail was an advertisement with a penny taped to it. Laughing and crying at the same time, I thanked the Lord. I had asked for just a little encouragement and that is exactly what He gave me.

That night at choir practice, the church administrator asked me to come by his office and pick up an envelope someone had dropped off for me. When I opened it up, there were seven one hundred-dollar bills. I asked who had left it and he said he had never seen her before. No one had known of our need and we never heard who the lady was or why she left us the money. Over the years, I cannot tell you how many times things like that happened.

As we give, we must remember the biblical motivation for giving is gratitude, a genuine thankfulness for what God has done in us and for us. We recognize that everything we have is from Him and we are merely caretakers, not owners. We should give freely because we have received freely (Matthew 10:8) knowing that God loves a cheerful giver (II Corinthians 9:7).

SERVANTHOOD PRECEDES USEFULNESS

One of the most incredible and distinguishing characteristics of the life of Christ was His servant spirit and His willingness to empty Himself in order to lift up sinful, undeserving, rebellious man. We are commanded to pattern our lives after Jesus in the same manner.

Our son, Frank III, had all kinds of difficulties as a baby. He was born with a tumor in his stomach, which required an operation when he was five weeks old. For the first few years of his life, he was sickly and it seemed he spent more time in the hospital than he did at home. When he was four, he was the size of a two-year-old. When he didn't learn to talk, we found out he was deaf; so he had an operation that restored his hearing and then he suffered through speech therapy. The whole ordeal left him very challenged. To top it all off, he was 15 months older and 15 months younger than his two sisters who seemed to do extremely well in everything. When he was a young boy, there was not an area in which he excelled and school work was especially difficult for him.

One night when he was in the fifth grade, I lost all patience. We'd gone over and over his school lesson and he still was not catching on. Finally I said, "Look, Frank, you just aren't getting it. I'm tired and you're tired; why don't you just go on to bed. We'll get up in the morning and maybe try again." I looked at his downcast face and knew what he was thinking, "You're giving up on me and you're my mom." But right then, in my frustration I couldn't handle it anymore, so I went to the kitchen and started washing dishes.

After a few minutes, I decided to go back to his room and pray with him. When I got outside his door, I heard his crying. Now ten-year-old boys do not sob like that. As I stood there it hit me, "You have just defeated him. He can't help that he has difficulty learning. The fruit of the Spirit is love, joy, peace, **patience**, etc. You aren't walking in the Spirit and as a result have devastated your little boy."

The great thing about the Lord is that we can always come to Him in repentance and receive His forgiveness. He restores us and puts us back in a place where He will use us. Right then I asked God to forgive me and give me an encouraging word for my young son. I thought of the verses in II Corinthians 12 when Paul asks God to remove a debilitating thorn. God's answer to him was "no," saying *"My grace is sufficient for you, for my power is made perfect in weakness."* As Paul considered this, he responded, *"Therefore I will boast all the more gladly about my weaknesses, so that Christ's power may rest on me. That is why, for Christ's sake, I delight in weaknesses, in insults, in hardships, in persecutions, in difficulties. For when I am weak, then I am strong."*

I went into the room and asked Frank to forgive me for not walking in the Spirit and losing patience with him. I told him what God had just taught me. Then I went on to say that God had given him a special gift in that He had put him in a place where he needed God's strength. His sisters would always be tempted to rely on themselves because they could, and as a result would miss a blessing if they were not careful. I told him to pray and thank the Lord that he had needs which made him rely on God.

The next morning we prayed together and asked for strength and wisdom. He clicked right through the material and went off to school to take the test. All during the day I prayed like crazy. That afternoon he came running out waving his paper saying, "Mama, Mama, I made a 100." He did not always make a perfect score after that, but the lessons he learned remained.

A few years later he became interested in magic, performing little tricks at backyard Bible clubs and various other places. One day he asked me to sew a cloth bag on a coat hanger, something that looked a little like a butterfly net, except it had a false lining. I made it up and gave it to him. A short time later he explained to me what he was going to do with it. "I will show the kids this bag and say, 'See, when you look at your life, you see nothing. But when God puts His hand in your life (he slipped his little hand into the bag's false lining and started pulling out all kinds of colorful scarves), He produces rich and wonderful things.'" Fighting back tears I said, "That's a good thing to teach."

Because of Frank III's medical problems when he was little, the doctors told us that there was a possibility that he would not graduate from high school. But through hard work and perseverance, he proved them wrong. So when it came time for him to get his diploma, there was not a happier or prouder mother anywhere. On the day of his senior honors convocation, I arrived early to get a seat which enabled me to watch him throughout the ceremony. It did not matter whether he would get any honors; I was just excited he was graduating. As they began announcing the award recipients I heard, "Honor student – Honors

Chemistry, Peggy Barker." Then, "Honor student – Honors English, Peggy Barker."

I looked over at my son's deflated face, reading his mind, "My little sister outdoes me again." This was supposed to be his day; he was the senior. I started praying that they would quit calling Peggy's name.

Then I prayed that God would show Frank that the world does not always honor the things that God honors. Right at that moment the principal rose to announce the valedictorian and salutatorian. I was stunned to hear him say, "We are a Christian school and it would be appropriate for us to honor what God honors. The distinguishing characteristic of the life and ministry of Christ was His servant attitude. Over the past four years we have had a student that exhibits true servanthood. Matthew 20:26b-28 says, *'whoever wants to become great among you must be your servant ,and whoever wants to be first must be your slave— just as the Son of Man did not come to be served, but to serve, and to give His life as a ransom for many.'*" He repeated verbatim the words I had just prayed. Then he went on to describe how this person helped the school and other students behind the scenes, always reaching out to the underdogs, setting up sound equipment, and preparing water bottles for the athletic teams. That day Frank III received the first annual Christian Service Award at Briarwood Christian High School. I would not have been prouder if he had been an All-American, All-Academic first string quarterback at Auburn University!

He went on to graduate from Samford University in mass communications and now serves as the Audio/Visual Director at Briarwood Presbyterian Church, continuing to live his life as a servant of Christ.

Living out Christ's pattern of humility, sacrifice, giving, and servanthood, motivated by genuine thankfulness, will set you apart from the world. And as a result God will be glorified. It will also bring you into an intimacy with God that cannot be described. You can trust Him because He will be faithful to His promises and will never leave you nor forsake you. Take it from me, you will never regret it.

MY PRAYER

Oh, God, teach me to have true humility that results from knowing Your great heart. Help me to esteem others as more deserving than I am. Help me not to seek great things for myself, but seek to build up others. I want to labor for the eternal and not for the temporary things that perish. Do not let me think like the world, but cause me to truly have the mind of Christ. Amen.

LOVE NOT THE WORLD

The world is full of lots of things
Upon which the joy of many hinge,
To have, to hold, and to control
Though such could never save the soul . . .

Those things for which men spend their lives
Those things to which their hearts are tied,
Are things of merely earthly gold
And none could ever save the soul . . .

For human praise and human prize
For things that lure and please the eyes;
For these men live, so we are told
Though such could never save the soul . . .

To be content, to be secure,
To please the flesh – no pain endure;
For such conformed to worldly mold
Though such could never save the soul . . .

To be the served, to hold first place,
To take the prize in every race,
To have my name engraved in gold
Could only mean I lose my soul. [3]

Notes

[1] Murray, Andrew, *Humility* (Fort Washington, Pennsylvania: Christian Literature Crusade, 1980), 15.

[2] Ibid, 14.

[3] Barker, Barbara B.

Chapter 3
PERSONAL APPLICATION

1. After reading this chapter, is there anything God is teaching you in one of these areas of your life?

    o   Humility
    o   Sacrifice
    o   Giving
    o   Serving

2. Believing that right actions follow right thinking, how should your actions change?

Chapter 3
BIBLE STUDY

Read Philippians 2:5-11. How is Christ's attitude described?

What do the following verses say about **humility**?
- Matthew 18:4
- Micah 6:8
- James 4:10
- I Peter 5:5-6

How does one learn humility?

Dying to self is a necessary process in the sanctification process.

What do you think it means to "take up the cross" (Matthew 16:24, Luke 14:27, Galatians 5:24)?

What happens when you "lose your life" according to Matthew 16:25?

Read Romans 12:1-2.
- What should be the motivation for our offering ourselves as "living sacrifices"?

- What makes a sacrifice acceptable to God?

- What is the result of offering ourselves in this way?

- What are some of the means that the world uses to conform our thinking, behavior, and values?

- What are some of the means of transformation?

What does the Bible say about **giving**?
- Matthew 6:19-21
- Luke 12:33
- Matthew 10:8
- II Corinthians 9:7
- Leviticus 27:30
- Malachi 3:10
- Malachi 3:8
- Proverbs 11:24
- Acts 20:35
- Luke 6:38

Servanthood is the requirement for being great. Read Matthew 20:26-28 and John 13:12-17. Paraphrase these passages in your own words.

How would you define serving? Whom should we serve?

What is the world's attitude toward serving?

According to Ephesians 6:7 what should be our motive in serving?

Chapter 3
DISCUSSION QUESTIONS

1. How are the attitudes we've just studied (humility, sacrifice, giving, and serving) interrelated?

2. Who is the most humble person you know? Why?

3. What are some practical ways you can put into practice the attitudes of dying to self and servanthood?

4. Discuss how one finds the balance between sacrificial giving and living in an affluent society.

CHAPTER 4

People Are More Important than Things

One day every one of us will stand before God and give account for our lives. What will we say? Where did we invest our lives? Was it in people, or in the accumulation of "stuff" and pursuit of self-indulgent activities? There are only two things in this world that will last forever: the Word of God and the souls of men. Would it only make sense to spend our time, effort, and resources in what will really last?

The apostle Paul endured stoning, beatings, arrests, shipwrecks, and all types of sufferings – all for the opportunity to share the Gospel message with others. He by no means had an easy life, primarily because he cared about others more than he cared about his own personal comfort. In his letter to the Thessalonians, Paul says he delighted in sharing not only the Gospel, but his very life (I Thessalonians 2:8) and he dealt with them like a father would his children, encouraging, comforting and urging them to live lives worthy of God (2:11-12). He worked night and day so that he would not be a burden to them (2:9). Then he says, *"For what is our hope, our joy, or crown in which we will glory in the presence of our Lord Jesus when he comes? Is it not you? Indeed, you are our glory and joy" (I Thessalonians 2:19-20)*. Oh, to have a heart for people like the apostle Paul!

When Frank and I married, we moved into a little house close to the church. The same house we have now; although, we have added on to it. All of our furniture was somebody's leftover made over, except for a beautiful Queen Anne coffee table my mother had given me. Loving that table, I always protected it very carefully when the high school students came over. One night we hosted a Bible study and our house was packed with teenagers. To make room for everyone, I had pushed the furniture back against the wall, securing the coffee table in the corner where no one could get to it. While the speaker was speaking, I looked across the room and, to my horror, saw a young man sitting on my coffee table. In the back pocket of his blue jeans was a pen with a clip. Every time he wiggled, the clip dug a scratch into my beautiful Queen Anne table. He was way across the room so I could not get to him. Each time the pen gouged into my precious table, I felt it cutting through my heart as well.

When everyone left, I broke down and cried. "Frank, I can't have anything that looks nice. It's just not fair."

He said, "Barbara, what is more important, the coffee table that is going to burn up or the kid sitting there whose soul is going on forever?" Unintentionally, he could make me feel so guilty. I had to give the right answer; even though, it was far from how I felt at that moment. But God worked the truth in my heart and I eventually believed it too. The lesson stays with me to this day. So when things get broken or lost or ruined, I think back to the boy on the coffee table and am instantly reminded of what is really important.

> ***Frank: "Barbara, what is more important, the coffee table that is going to burn up or the kid sitting there whose soul is going on forever?"***

We must see everything from God's eternal perspective and value what He values. What difference will a "trinket" make a hundred years from now? What will we wish we had done with our lives when we look back? I guarantee we will not wish we had accumulated more stuff.

Matthew 6:19-21 instructs us not to store up (invest in) treasure on earth because it does not last. Instead, we should store up true treasure in heaven. How do we do that? By investing in the spiritual welfare of others.

An illustration has been given of a very wealthy Christian lady who spent most of her time on this earth in self-indulging activities. The day came when she died and was being ushered to her permanent home in heaven. As she and her heavenly escort walked the golden streets, she saw huge, gorgeous mansions on either side of the street. "Would that beautiful mansion possibly be mine," she inquired of the angel.

"Unfortunately, no, that one belongs to your pastor," was the reply.

"Oh," she said, her voice thick with disappointment.

"What about that one? I love it!"

"No, that one belongs to your grocer."

Sadly she said, "I can't begrudge him for it. He was such a giving man when he was on earth. There is no telling how much free food he gave away to those who needed it."

The next gorgeous house, she was told, belonged to her former yard man.

"If this is his, I can't wait to see mine," she said excitedly.

Finally they turned a corner and stopped in front of a little shanty.

Horrified, the lady said, "This one can't possibly be mine."

Her escort said, "I'm sorry. We did the best we could with what you sent up."

I don't know about you, but that little illustration makes me sit back and think about how I invest my time and resources here on earth.

Paul expounds on this lesson of investing in eternal things: *"In this way they will lay up treasure for themselves as a firm foundation for the coming age, so that they may take hold of the life that is truly life" (I Timothy 6:19)*. When we invest our resources in what really matters, we not only prepare for the future, but we learn what true life is all about. Scripture teaches us, and my experience has proven, that the sacrificial lifestyle is much fuller and more abundant than any kind of self-indulgent one.

In the parable of the talents in Matthew 25:14-30, Christ challenges us to be good stewards with the resources He entrusts to us. The faithful servants who invested their talents were rewarded, but the one who hid his talent was thrown into the darkness. Being a co-laborer with Christ means that I take all He gives me and invest it in such a way so as to produce the greatest return. His Holy Spirit guides me as to exactly how to do that. This parable teaches that there are rewards for those who invest wisely and severe consequences for those who do not.

I would be remiss if I did not talk about living a balanced life. How we apply these principles in our own lives is as individual as our personal walks with Him. God does not call all of us to sell everything and live on beans in an old shack. But He does call every one of us to lay everything we have at the foot of His cross and ask Him to use it for His purposes. And as we do this, we must remember that He is the source of all our resources and He blesses us in order to equip us to be a blessing to others. As the pastor from Watts, Los Angeles Dr. E. V. Hill once said, "When God blesses you, He seldom has you in mind."

E. V. Hill: When God blesses you, He seldom has you in mind.

Being faithful for the opportunities God brings our way is not always easy or pleasant. One Saturday night we received a call from a man who said, "Is this Preacher Barkley?"

Frank said, "This is Frank Barker."

"We heard you take in people. We don't have no place to stay, so we need you to come get us."

It turned out that because this couple had not paid the rent, their boarding house had thrown all of their things on the street. While sweet Frank went to pick them up, I prepared their supper and moved little Frank out of his room onto the sofa. His room was the one we always used for guests. Although usually very compliant, this night as he took his pillow and moved onto the living room couch, he grumbled, "When I grow up, I am going to write a book called *Where Am I Going to Sleep Tonight, Mama?*"

When they arrived, I put their dinner on the table. The wife was a very large woman with high heels and bleached blonde hair. It appeared she had been poured into a pair of polyester pants. Throughout the evening, she kept her head down and would not look at anyone. Her husband, whom she cowered behind, was a little man with a really bright smile and was very thankful for all that we did. Frank led the man to the Lord that night and then we all went to bed.

The next morning Frank was going out of town, so he asked me to take the husband to a gas station run by a friend who hired people on a daily basis. That left the wife for me to entertain. However, I had planned to go with my friends to hear a Christian speaker and then on to a nice restaurant for lunch.

Rarely getting time away from the children, I was looking forward to it.

I told the wife, who I discovered was pregnant, "I know you want to rest, so you can stay here." My real reason was not for her comfort, but for my convenience. I knew she would not fit in with my friends. It soon became obvious she was going to cling to me as she did to her husband and wanted no part of staying at home by herself. So we left for the meeting with my resenting it all the way. Inside my conversation with God went like this, "Every time I get a chance to have fun, something happens." I was a pitiful martyr all the way there.

As I got out of the car at the church, I heard God say very clearly to my heart, *"I was not ashamed to call them brothers" (Hebrews 2:11).* I realized Jesus was not ashamed of me. When I thought about it, the difference between that woman and me was miniscule, compared to the difference between Christ and me. How could I look at her with disgust when God looks on me with such tenderness and compassion? So I grabbed her by the arm and walked proudly into the church, prepared to judge all of my friends who looked down on her. Oh well, two steps forward, one step backwards.

After Frank got back, he took them down to a local mission where the man got a job. They worked as staff for several years and his conversion proved to be genuine.

One day when you stand before the Lord He will ask, "What have you done with your life? Did you invest your time and resources in people or things?"

How will you respond? I long to hear the words: *"Well done, good and faithful servant! You have been faithful with a few things; I will put you in charge of many things. Come and share your master's happiness!" (Matthew 25:21).*

MY PRAYER

Dear Lord, I long to have a heart for people like the apostle Paul. Help me to see them as You do and love them even when it requires sacrifice. I am humbled by all the resources, talents, and opportunities you have entrusted to me. I give total control of them to You. Give me wisdom for how to invest them for the advancement of Your Kingdom – for Your glory. Help me to remember that life is not about me, but You. I thank You for giving me the great privilege of working with You in Your kingdom. Amen.

Chapter 4
PERSONAL APPLICATION

1. What do you see as your purpose in life and how is that supported in your actions?

2. Name three resources or talents that God has entrusted to you.

3. How are you investing each of them?

4. How can you do a better job of using each of them for the advancement of God's kingdom?

Chapter 4
BIBLE STUDY

Read Ephesians 2:10. How are Christians God's workmanship? Also, refer to Psalm 139:14-16 and Jeremiah 1:5.

What good works does God want us to do?

Describe Paul's love for the Christians in Thessalonica (I Thessalonians 2:6-12, 19-20).

When you genuinely love someone you share not only the Gospel, but also your life. How do you share your life with someone?

How can you be a burden to others?

What was Paul's motive behind his relationship with the Thessalonians (2:6, 8, 12, 19-20)?

What does Paul say in verse 10 about how he lived his life before them?

What impresses you most about this passage in I Thessalonians? How does it change how you relate to others?

Where does love for others come from (I Thessalonians 3:12)?

Who is our example of how to love others (John 15:12)?

Therefore, how should we follow His example?

What is one result of loving others (John 13:35)?

Chapter 4
DISCUSSION QUESTIONS

1. If you were to die today, what would be the epitaph on your gravestone?

2. What attitudes strengthen materialism's grip?

3. What attitudes weaken its grip?

4. How are you intentionally investing in the lives of other people?

5. What have been the costs and rewards of this investment?

CHAPTER 5

Finding Fulfillment
in God Alone

Man's great downfall is that he is continually seeking elsewhere for those things that only God can give. He seeks for satisfaction and fulfillment in human relationships, material security, personal accomplishments, the praise of man, physical beauty and strength, and even the government. Great sacrifices in the pursuit of personal pleasure are made under the delusion that ultimately, when the illusive goal is obtained, there will be fulfillment. His failure to find joy and contentment in these things, or to have his deepest needs met in the pursuit of them, leads to frantic lives, frustration, insecurity, restlessness, and bad choices.

God never intended for these temporal things to satisfy the hunger of man's soul. Pascal, the great mathematician, said that in every man there is a God-shaped vacuum which can only be filled with God Himself. Jesus said, *"I have come that they may have life, and have it to the full" (John 10:10a) and "I have told you this so that my joy may be in you and that your joy may be complete" (John 15:11).* Paul prayed in Ephesians 3:19 that his readers would be, *"filled with all the fullness of God."*

When we are filled with God, we have no need for other "fillings." God created us for a relationship with Himself. He wanted us to know that He is our God, our Rock and Salvation, Father, Husband, and the Lover of our souls. He promises that:

- His provision is adequate for every need – *"And my God will meet all your needs according to his glorious riches in Christ Jesus" (Philippians 4:19),*
- His grace is sufficient for all our weaknesses – *"My grace is sufficient for you, for my power is made perfect in weakness" (I Corinthians 12:9a),*
- His peace is perfect for all of our trials – *"You will keep in perfect peace him whose mind is steadfast, because he trusts in you" (Isaiah 26:3),*
- His will is trustworthy in all of our circumstances – *"And we know that in all things God works for the good of those who love him, who have been called according to his purpose" (Romans 8:28),* and
- His wisdom is always available – *"If any of you lacks wisdom, he should ask God, who gives generously to all without finding fault, and it will be given to him" (James 1:5).*

The biggest challenge in attaining fulfillment in God alone is confusing our **needs** with our **wants** and **desires**. When desires become expectations, we are disappointed, turn from God, and search for fulfillment in other ways. We come under the delusion that what we want will bring fulfillment, instead of the God Who created us.

How do we distinguish between needs and desires? **Needs** may be defined as those things necessary for our existence which are:

- To be **R**edeemed from the consequences of sin, which is spiritual death. We need spiritual life because without it we would be doomed to an eternity in hell. *"For God so loved the world, that he gave his one and only Son, that whoever believes in him shall not perish, but have everlasting life" (John 3:16).*

- To have a **R**eason for living. We need purpose. Paul tells us in Philippians 1:21, *"For to me to live is Christ, and to die is gain."* And this purpose for living can only be found through a relationship with Christ.

- To have **R**elationship. Man was created to have a relationship with God. That is why there is always a sense of void when this relationship does not exist. *"I will live with them and walk among them, and I will be their God, and they will be my people" (II Corinthians 6:16b).*

- To have the **R**equirements of the physical life met, e.g., shelter, clothing, air, water, and food. *"So do not worry, saying, 'What shall* *we eat?' or 'What shall we drink?' or 'What shall we wear?' For the pagans run after all these things, and your heavenly Father knows that you need them. But seek first his kingdom and his righteousness, and all these things will be given to you as well" (Matthew 6:31-33).*

- To have **R**efuge from all that threatens one's security, both physically and spiritually. *"So we say with confidence, 'The Lord is my helper; I will not be afraid. What can man do to me?'" (Hebrews 13:6). "A righteous man may have many troubles, but the Lord delivers him from them all" (Psalm 34:19).*

A lady who knew how to distinguish needs from desires was Laura. She helped my mama raise my sisters and me and then helped me with my children when they were little. She lived downtown close to the interstate in a small house next door to a vacant lot which was used as a dump. She had cleaned out a little plot and planted a garden. During the day while she was at work, bums, who lived on welfare, would steal her vegetables. It made me so mad, but she just said that they needed the food more than she did. After all, she had plenty to eat. Every time I picked her up and asked how she was, she responded, "Oh, Miss Barbara, I am saved and kept by the power of God and so grateful for a portion of my health and strength. God don't owe me a crust of bread or a drink of water, but He give me my breakfast today. Oh, God is so good!" She was a true picture of one totally fulfilled in God and is now enjoying the rewards of a well-lived life in heaven with her precious Savior.

When **we** seek to meet our needs from sources other than God, we will never be truly satisfied. We will not be filled or fulfilled. Scripture identifies those "sources" as broken, leaky fountains, which can never quench the thirst of His people. *"My people have committed two sins: they have forsaken me, the spring of living water, and have dug their own cisterns, broken cisterns that cannot hold water" (Jeremiah 2:13).* Water in this verse represents spiritual nourishment. Jesus told the woman at the well (John 4:4-14) that He was the Living Water and *"whoever drinks the water I give him will never thirst."* Psalm 1 expounds on this by saying that the man who delights and mediates on the Word is like a *"a tree planted by streams of water, which yields its fruit in season and whose leaf does not wither, whatever he does prospers."*

Why is it that we continually try to find our satisfaction in material possessions, personal pleasures, accomplishments, or relationships, forsaking the Fountain of Living Water? First of all, we do not believe the promises of God given to us in His Word. Secondly, deep down we think that God is withholding something that is good. Thirdly, we want to be in control. We want what **we** want, **when** we want it. We think we know what is best. And lastly, we want to be exalted and glorified instead of God.

Sometimes we are not patient with the timing of God's provision. As we wait on God's provision, we can become discouraged and distracted and succumb to the enemy's fiery darts which attack the character of God. We must remember that many times God delays so that we will trust only in Him. It has been said that God is never late, but seldom early. Even in His delays, He will be glorified.

God is never late, but seldom early.

To be fulfilled in God alone, we must cease striving with our Maker and yield our needs and desires to Him. We must realize that He created us in such a way that our satisfaction and identity can only come from our relationship with Him.

Prayer is a key element in this relationship. He has told us not to be anxious about anything, but to make **all** our requests and desires known to Him (Philippians 4:6). We trust Him to answer our prayers as He sees fit for our good and His glory. We rely on His precious promise that as we seek His Kingdom **first** all these things will be added to us (Matthew 6:33).

How is this fulfillment realized in our lives? We must have faith in who God **is** (the sum total of all of His attributes) and trust that He will be true to His character and meet our needs as He promised. Abraham is an example of this faith. We read in Romans 4:20-21 that he did not *"waver through unbelief regarding the promise of God, but was strengthened in his faith and gave glory to God, being fully persuaded that God had power to do what he had promised."*

How do we have that kind of faith? *"Faith comes by hearing the message and the message is heard through the Word of Christ" (Romans 10:17).* We exercise faith through the study and application of Scripture to our lives, bringing every thought into captivity to His Word (II Corinthians 10:5b), and aligning our thoughts with God's truth.

Faith grows stronger as we exercise it, when we practice obedience to the light we have been given. Just like with our diets, the more we discipline ourselves to eat the right kinds of food, the less appetite we have for the nutritional-lacking fluff. As we exercise and feed spiritual muscles, they will become stronger.

Simply put, fulfillment in God comes when we think right and do right. As the old hymn summarizes, "Trust and obey, for there's no other way to be happy in Jesus, but to trust and obey."

TRUST AND OBEY
By John H. Sammis

When we walk with the Lord
in the light of His word,
what a glory He sheds on our way!
While we do His good will,
He abides with us still,
and with all who will trust and obey.

Refrain:
Trust and obey, for there's no other way
to be happy in Jesus, but to trust and obey.

Not a burden we bear,
not a sorrow we share,
but our toil He doth richly repay;
not a grief or a loss,
not a frown or a cross,
but is blest if we trust and obey.
(Refrain)

But we never can prove
the delights of His love
until all on the altar we lay;
for the favor He shows,
for the joy He bestows,
are for them who will trust and obey.
(Refrain)

Then in fellowship sweet
we will sit at His feet,
or we'll walk by His side in the way;
what He says we will do,
where He sends we will go;
never fear, only trust and obey.
(Refrain)[1]

MY PRAYER

Dear God, I pray that I would be totally and completely focused on You and trust in Your ability to meet my needs. I want to be totally fulfilled with You. I pray for the faith to trust you in all areas of my life. I love you! Amen.

Notes

[1] Words by John H. Sammis (http://www.hymnsite.com/lyrics/umh467.sht, accessed 1/26/07).

Chapter 5
PERSONAL APPLICATION

1. Is there an area of your life in which you are looking for fulfillment in some place other than God? It could be in finances, relationships, work, etc.

2. List and describe how God has met your needs.

3. After reading this chapter, have you reclassified some of your needs to wants?

4. Are there any unfulfilled desires that you need to give over to God?

5. When have you been successful in trusting God to be your fulfillment?

Chapter 5
BIBLE STUDY

At the beginning of King Solomon's reign, God told Solomon he could have anything he asked for. What was Solomon's response (I Kings 3:6-9)?

What was God's response to Solomon (I Kings 3:10-14)?

King Solomon wrote the book of Ecclesiastes toward the end of his reign. In what things had he tried to find fulfillment?
- 1:3
- 1:13
- 2:1, 10
- 2:3
- 2:4
- 2:8
- 2:9

In all of these pursuits, what was his conclusion (Ecclesiastes 12:8)?

According to Solomon, how can one not be distracted by the blessings God provides (5:19-20)?

What is Solomon's conclusion from his mistakes (12:13-14)?

How does God feel about His people and how is it demonstrated?
- Jeremiah 31:3
- Zephaniah 3:17
- Romans 5:8
- Romans 8:35-39
- I John 3:1

According to the following verses, what are the provisions of God?
- Jeremiah 31:13
- Jeremiah 31:1
- Hebrews 13:6
- Colossians 2:9-10
- Isaiah 58:11
- Psalm 103:5
- Psalm 73:23-24

What is the source of my wants (desires) and how are they obtained (Psalm 37:4)?

What does the Bible say about God's purposes for man?
- Isaiah 43:10
- Isaiah 43:21

What do you learn about faith from the following verses?

- Hebrews 11:1
- Hebrews 11:6
- Luke 17:5-6
- Romans 10:17
- Galatians 5:6
- James 2:17
- Ephesians 6:16
- James 1:6

Chapter 5
DISCUSSION QUESTIONS

1. What does a God-shaped vacuum feel like? Has there been a time in your life when everything was going great and you still felt like something was lacking?

2. Describe a time when you confused a want with a need.

3. Share a time when you did not think God was going to meet your need. What was the result?

4. What advice would you give to another Christian who is not trusting God to be his or her fulfillment?

CHAPTER 6

Developing the Attitude of Gratitude

The Bible instructs us to *"give thanks in all circumstances, for this is God's will for you in Christ Jesus" (1 Thessalonians 5:18)*. This verse says to give thanks in **all** things, not just in the good things. The joy we experience in life is directly proportional to our thankfulness. And thankfulness is a choice.

Lack of a grateful spirit can have devastating results. God tells us that part of the reason for the downward spiral of sin in a person's life is not being thankful. *"For although they knew God, they neither glorified him as God **nor gave thanks to him**, but their thinking became futile and their foolish hearts were darkened" (Romans 1:21, emphasis added)*. If you continue reading in Romans 1, you will see the very disturbing consequences of futile thinking and darkened hearts when God gives people over to their sinful desires. It is not pretty.

I believe that the very first sin in the Garden of Eden originated from Eve's lack of thankfulness. What was she thinking? She had it all: a home in Eden, the breathtakingly beautiful place God designed, with a perfect, sinless husband. Even better, she had a special relationship with God, unhindered by a sinful nature.

Instead of resting in and appreciating all that God had provided, Eve, as the prey of Satan, easily shifted her focus to what she could not have. Her lack of thankfulness caused her to question God's goodness and opened the door for Satan's deceit.

Isn't that what we all do? Instead of being thankful for what we have, we blame God for not giving us what we want. I know single girls who are not thankful for God's provisions in their lives and think that happiness is dependent on having a husband. And I have married friends who complain about their husband's flaws instead of appreciating their husbands' good qualities. These are just two examples. In spite of all of the spiritual and material blessings that we experience, unfortunately, we can be a very ungrateful and discontented people.

An ungrateful spirit is evidenced by grumbling and complaining. God has some very specific things to say about this particular sin. When He miraculously delivered the Israelites from slavery in Egypt, He provided for their every need on their trek through the wilderness. I am not saying they had an easy trip, but God was with them. Instead of being thankful and trusting Him, they complained about what they did not have. Time after time God gave them what they requested, but it did not take very long before they were griping again. The Lord was angry with their attitude and punished them. A vicious circle began of blessings, complaining, consequences, and repentance. That vicious circle continues even today.

Jesus and Paul were not pleased with complainers either. *"Stop grumbling among yourselves,"* Jesus said in John 6:43. And Paul warned the Philippians in 2:14-16, *"Do everything without complaining or arguing, so that you may become blameless and pure, children of God without fault in a crooked and depraved generation, in which you shine like stars in the universe as you hold out the word of life."*

Ingratitude not only brings on God's wrath, it robs of spiritual blessings that God desires to give. Why should He entrust you with more, when you are not even grateful for what He has given you?

I was raised in an affluent home where my father could supply us with everything we could want or need; even though, in his wisdom he did not. He always said, "I would do you a grave disservice if I gave you more than you have the capacity to appreciate." Growing up, my thankfulness was the barometer that determined how much of his abundance I enjoyed.

> ***My father always said,***
> ***"I would do you a grave disservice***
> ***if I gave you more than you have***
> ***the capacity to appreciate."***

When you choose to be thankful, the place to start is with your relationship with Christ and

His provisions for you. Here are just a few from Ephesians 1. He chose you before creation to be holy and blameless in His sight, having redeemed you by the blood of His Son and adopted you as His child. He made known to you the mystery of His will and marked you with a seal, which is His Holy Spirit. The truth is when you have Christ, you need nothing else. As the hymn says, "Turn your eyes upon Jesus. Look full in His wonderful face. And the things of earth will grow strangely dim, in the light of His glory and grace."[1]

The next step is to learn to contemplate on the attributes of God: His wisdom, holiness, justice, mercy, compassion, sovereignty, and omniscience, to name a few. The most incredible aspect of His character is His everlasting love (Jeremiah 31:3) and His desire to satisfy His people with His goodness (Jeremiah 31:14). He is a good God and wants the best for us. *"Which of you, if his son asks for bread, will give him a stone? Or if he asks for a fish, will give him a snake? If you, then, though you are evil, know how to give good gifts to your children, how much more will your Father in heaven give good gifts to those who ask him!" (Matthew 7:9-11)*.

The greatest demonstration of His love is that *"while we were still sinners, Christ died for us" (Romans 5:8)*. And if the ultimate expression of God's love was the giving of His own Son to bear the sin-debt of man, then what lesser need would God leave unmet? *"He who did not spare his own Son, but gave him up for us all – how will he not also, along with him, graciously give us all things?"*

(Romans 8:32). Man's greatest need was supplied by God's greatest gift.

Man's greatest need was supplied by God's greatest gift.

Not only does God love you, He controls everything that affects you. In Matthew 10:28-31 Jesus says, *"Do not be afraid of those who kill the body but cannot kill the soul. Rather, be afraid of the one who can destroy both soul and body in hell. Are not two sparrows sold for a penny? Yet not one of them will fall to the ground apart from the will of your Father. And even the very hairs of your head are all numbered. So don't be afraid; you are worth more than many sparrows."* Other Scriptures that reinforce this promise are: *"Have you not heard? Long ago I ordained it. In days of old I planned it; now I have brought it to pass . . ." (Isaiah 37:26);* and *" . . . we know that in all things God works for the good of those who love him, who have been called according to his purpose" (Romans 8:28)*. This verse in Romans does not say that all things in and of themselves are good from man's perspective, but that He is working all things **together** for good. And the "good" toward which "all things are working," according to Romans 8:29, is that you are being conformed to the image of Christ, which is God's ultimate goal for every believer. The Amplified version of Philippians 3:10 says, *"For my determined purpose is that I may know him – that I may progressively become more deeply and intimately acquainted with him, perceiving and recog-*

nizing and understanding the wonders of his Person more strongly and more clearly. And that I may in that same way, come to know the power outflowing from his resurrection, which it exerts over believers; and that I may so share his sufferings as to be continually transformed in spirit into his likeness even to his death."

Based on these truths, you should be able to say with all of your heart, "If I have Him, I have it all." How well this is expressed by the hymn writer, Harriet E. Buell:

My Father is rich in houses and lands,
He holdeth the wealth of the world in His
    hands!
Of rubies and diamonds, of silver and gold,
His coffers are full, He has riches untold.

Refrain
I'm a child of the King,
A child of the King:
With Jesus my Savior,
I'm a child of the King.

My Father's own Son, the Savior of men,
Once wandered on earth as the poorest of
    them;
But now He is pleading our pardon on high,
That we may be His when He comes by and by.

I once was an outcast stranger on earth,
A sinner by choice, an alien by birth,
But I've been adopted, my name's written
    down,
An heir to a mansion, a robe and a crown.

A tent or a cottage, why should I care?
They're building a palace for me over
    there;
Though exiled from home, yet still may I
    sing:
All glory to God; I'm a child of the King. [2]

Thirdly, you must realize that God does not owe you anything except judgment. The very air you breathe is a gift. We are all born sinners, having no hope. Our sin creates a great, insurmountable enmity between God and us. Romans 3:10-18 tells us that there is no one who is good. Jesus, the Righteous One, is God's standard of "goodness" and compared to Him there are no "good" people. Everyone deserves His wrath, but instead Christians receive His free gift of compassion. *"Because of the Lord's great love we are not consumed, for his compassions never fail. They are new every morning; great is your faithfulness" (Lamentations 3:22-23).*

Fourthly, keep in mind the whole reason for your existence. You are God's workmanship created for His purposes, not your own (Ephesians 2:10). According to the Shorter Catechism, the chief end of man is to "glorify God and enjoy Him forever." Somehow, man has turned that around to believe that the chief end of God is to glorify man. This attitude is the seedbed for ingratitude and bears the fruit of self-centered and self-absorbed behavior.

Fifthly, you must realize that being thankful is an act of your will. I Thessalonians 5:18 tells us to **give** thanks in all circumstances. It doesn't say to **feel** thankful. Thankfulness does not come naturally and must be learned. How? By resting in the realization that God loves you and controls everything that happens to you. Make an effort to be thankful for every single thing in your life. Start off with the little things, like the beauty of the world around you. Offer up thanks-givings to God as you walk through each day. Thank Him that you have food to eat and a place to sleep. Begin making a list of the things that you are thankful for. When you are in a down-and-out mood, refer back to them. Write down the hard things and thank God for them too. You may not **feel** thankful, but you are being obedient by an act of your will. Proverbs tell us, *"As a man thinks in his heart, so is he."* As you **practice** thankfulness, you will **be** thankful.

Lastly, verbalize your thankfulness to others. Not only will gratitude become more natural, your attitude will overflow into their lives. In contrast, observe how many times conversations around you drift to the negative. "My, it sure is hot today (or cold, or rainy)." "I am so tired. My baby kept me up all night." By voicing thanksgiving you can be a change agent in others' lives. Before you know it, negative talk will decrease.

On one occasion Frank went to Korea, leaving the three children and me with $15. As I dropped him off at the airport I asked, "What am I going to do? How will we make it?"

"Honey, just pray." He left and I was mad. How could he do that to me? Of course, we never had any money and we always had to trust God to meet our needs, but I just felt safer when he was there praying with me.

During the week, a friend from church came over to show me the new dress she bought at a real bargain price. I thought to myself, "I wish I had the money you spent on that dress to buy groceries." One of my dear friends called later and said she was going to the grocery store and asked if she could pick up anything for me. Feeling like a pitiful martyr, I told her that I did not need anything. It was true I did not really **need** anything, but there were a lot of things I wanted – like some food.

One evening, after five nights of Cream of Wheat (the only food we had in the house), I stood at the stove stirring the pot, complaining to God about our situation, when it suddenly dawned on me, "How many mothers in the world would give anything to feed their children a bowl of Cream of Wheat every night?" I glanced into the den and saw my three healthy children reading textbooks from their Christian school. And then I turned on the faucet and clean water came out. I was overwhelmed at how much I had to be thankful for. Most of the world would trade places with me in a heartbeat. It was one of those moments that will stick with me forever. I seemed to hear God say, "Barbara, you are only thankful after you reach your 'have-to-have' level. True thanksgiving begins with the breath you breathe." The week passed; we still had the $15, all of our needs were met, and I had learned a very valuable lesson on gratitude.

> *"Barbara, you are only thankful*
> *after you reach your "have-to-have" level.*
> *True thanksgiving begins with the breath*
> *you breathe."*

Contentment is the disposition that results from a thankful attitude. In *The Rare Jewel of Christian Contentment*, Jeremiah Burroughs, a Puritan, defined Christian contentment like this: "Christian contentment is that sweet, inward, quiet, gracious frame of spirit, which freely submits to and delights in God's wise and fatherly disposal in every condition."[3] Taking liberties with this great quote, I have elaborated it slightly to say: "Contentment is the sweet, settled disposition of acceptance, **with** gratitude, **from** God's hand, **whatever** circumstances or provision **He** has ordained for me. This is done acknowledging that in His love, wisdom, and sovereign power, He orders the lives of His own. Then trusting in His ability to provide for them in such a way that advances their greatest good and His greatest glory, one can rest in the full assurance of His care and keeping."

One night I was praising God for all my blessings: for my wonderful husband, sweet children, and healthy body. My thoughts immediately went to the persecuted Christians throughout the world. This same good God, Who had provided safe and pleasant pastures for me, was at the same time allowing those people to go through horrors that I could not comprehend. We must remember that God is good and His goodness is not determined by the particular enjoyable things He brings into our lives. God is good not because of what He does, but whatever He does is good because He is good. We give thanks to Him in **all** things, good or bad, because they are **His** will concerning **us**.

> *God is good not because of what*
> *He does, but whatever He does*
> *is good because He is good.*

In the early days, there was a lady at Briarwood who really got on Frank's nerves. She was constantly telling him what he was doing wrong. He tried to avoid her, but no matter where he went, she found him. It got so bad that he prayed for God to remove her. God spoke back to him very clearly, "No. She is My instrument in your life to give you the opportunity to know grace, patience, and love." He remembered Paul when he asked God to remove his "thorn in the flesh." God had told Paul, "*'My grace is sufficient for you for my power is made perfect in weakness.' Therefore I will boast all the more gladly about my weaknesses, so that Christ's power may rest on me*" *(II Corinthians 12:9)*. From that point on, instead of grumbling when he saw her, he started silently saying, "Thank you, Lord, for my thorn."

God can, in His sovereignty, change people or circumstances, open doors, and close doors. But He may choose not to in order to accomplish His purposes in your life. Our oldest daughter, Anita, was a cheerleader when she was at Auburn — the cutest, sweetest one they ever had, I must add. When the games were broadcast on television, the cameramen seemed to love her because she was always the one they focused on. Anita would say, "Oh, Mama, that's just because I am the little one on the end." I knew better. Anyway, when she tried out the second year, I prayed for God to have His will with the tryouts, knowing that, of course, she would get it.

She made it all the way to the last round, but was chosen as an alternate. Her heart was broken, but having released the results to God beforehand, she thanked the Lord under her breath when the announcement was made. Late the next night, she received a call from Auburn's spirit captain, the one who had announced the newly chosen cheerleading squad. He asked if he could come over and talk with her. When they got together, the young man wanted to know what she had said when her name was announced as alternate. She told him that she had thanked the Lord, because having asked for His will, her getting alternate must have been what He wanted.

"Why did you say that?" he said.

She replied, "Because God is my Father and gives me only His best." She spent the next two hours sharing Christ with him.

When tryouts came around again the next year, she did not have much hope of being chosen. The emphasis had gone more toward gymnastics and she was not a gymnast. Not wanting others to think she was resentful toward the previous year's decision, she went ahead and tried out anyway. Lo and behold she made it! I told her, "Anita, when God wants you somewhere, it does not matter what your qualifications are. He will open the door. And when He does not want you somewhere, it does not matter how capable you are, you will not get it." That is one of the great things about trusting God. There is nothing He cannot do and nothing He cannot provide. Contentment comes when we have total confidence that He is in control of every single thing that concerns us.

O THIRSTY ONE
(written after hearing Frank's sermons on Isaiah 55)

O, thirsty one, come now partake!
A promise sure with you I make.
I long to satisfy your soul;
I long to cleanse and make you whole.
I would fulfill your heart's desire
And set your weary soul afire,
And pour my Spirit's power through you.
Reveal My love in all I do.
My grace sufficient you will know;
My faithfulness with you will go.

My ways are not your ways, I know.
For you, like sheep astray would go.
But I did take the debt you owed;
The path to Heaven I have shown.
I've spoken words that you may trust,
If you obey and put Me first.

But you must seek with all your heart
And from your wicked ways depart
So, thirsty one, come hear My call—
Drink deep of Me, your All-in-All!! [4]

MY PRAYER

Dear Lord, I want to be a thankful person. Help me to see life from your perspective, die to my own selfishness, and live for you. Please guard my mouth and keep me from complaining. Show me areas in which I am not thankful so that I may give those areas to You and trust in your loving control of them. I want to be thankful for even the very hard things because I know that You will work them together for good in my life. I love you. Amen.

Notes

[1] Words and music by Helen H. Lemmel, 1922, (http://www. cyberhymnal.org/htm/t/u/turnyour.htm, accessed 12/21/06).

[2] Words by Harriet E. Buell, (http://www.faithalone.org/journal/ 1999ii/J22-99f.htm, accessed 12/21/06).

[3] Burroughs, Jeremiah; *The Rare Jewel of Christian Contentment*, (Wilmington, Delaware: Sovereign Grace Publishers), 2.

[4] Barker, Barbara B.

Chapter 6
PERSONAL APPLICATION

1. What is there in your life that you cannot genuinely thank God for? Why? The Bible instructs us to be thankful in **all** things (I Thessalonians 5:18).

2. How is your ingratitude related to your expectation of what you think you deserve?

3. Is your conversation peppered with thanksgiving or complaining?

4. How do you express your gratitude to God?

5. What is the relationship between gratitude and contentment?

6. How would you rate your contentment in the following areas?

    • Material possessions
    • Station in life
    • Looks
    • Relationships

7. How does your thinking need to change in order to become content in these areas?

Chapter 6
BIBLE STUDY

Let's take a look at the Israelites after they were rescued from their slavery in Egypt.

Read the following verses and for each instance describe the difficulty they experienced, their reaction, and God's response.
- Exodus 15:24, 27
- Exodus 16:2-3, 11
- Numbers 14:2-3, 27-29

Based on your study, what do you learn about how God views complaining?

Read Psalm 106:21 and 24-27.
- What preceded the Israelites grumbling?

- Where were they when they grumbled?

- What did they do after they grumbled?

- What was God's reaction?

There is a difference in grumbling and complaining and voicing your questions and concerns to God. Now let's look at another person who encountered an unpleasant, impossible situation. To give you a little background, Habakkuk expressed his deep concern to God about the evil around in his nation of Judah. God's answer was surprising: I'm going to use the evil nation of Babylon to punish the evildoers in the land.

- What was Habakkuk's complaint (Habakkuk 1:2-3)?

- What was God's answer to Habakkuk's prayer (1:5-6)? Was this the answer that Habakkuk had hoped for?

- What did he do after he expressed his concerns to God (2:1)?

- Read Habakkuk 3:2, 4, 6. How did Habakkuk differ from the Israelites as to viewing God's attributes and provisions?

- What is the difference between how the Israelites and Habakkuk brought their concerns to God (3:16b)? Note: the answer has to do with surrendering the will.

- What were Habakkuk's final comments and how did they reflect his relationship with God (3:17-19)?

What does the Bible say about gratitude/ thankfulness?
- Psalm 28:7
- Psalm 35:18
- Psalm 50:23
- Philippians 4:6
- Colossians 3:15
- I Thessalonians 5:18
- Hebrews 12:28

How did these people exhibit gratitude?
- David (I Chronicles 29:10-14)
- Jonah (Jonah 2:9), Where was he when he expressed his gratitude (2:1)?
- The Leper (Luke 17:11-19)

What are some of the things that Paul thanks God for?
- II Thessalonians 2:13
- Philippians 1:3
- I Corinthians 15:57
- II Corinthians 2:14

What did the apostle Paul say about contentment?
- Philippians 4:11-13
- I Timothy 6:6
- I Timothy 6:8

Read Hebrews 13:5. When you are content what are you free from? What promise from God helps us be content?

Paul had a "thorn in the flesh" that he asked God to take away. God said no. What was Paul's response (II Corinthians 12:7-10)?

What should be your perspective in difficult circumstances (II Corinthians 4:17-18)?

Ultimately, contentment comes down to submitting your will to the will of a loving, powerful, all-knowing Father. When faced with a painful, agonizing death, what was Jesus' prayer (Matthew 26:39)?

Chapter 6
DISCUSSION QUESTIONS

1. What did you learn in the Bible Study section contrasting the Israelites and Habakkuk on how they expressed their concerns and displeasure to God?

2. How is your view of God related to your attitude of gratitude?

3. In what specific ways can you become a more thankful person?

4. How is the best way to handle a person who is complaining, without appearing to be judgmental or self-righteous?

5. How can you be sincerely thankful for the hard things of life?

6. In what ways do you encourage discontentment in others? How can you encourage contentment in others? Be specific.

7. What is the difference between contentment and lethargy? Discuss the balance between ambition and contentment. How is balance obtained?

CHAPTER 7

You Are Essential in the Body of Christ

All of the descriptions in Scripture used to describe Christians are "collectives": kingdom, nation, body, building, etc. A collective is a unit comprised of many parts, called to one purpose, subject to one authority, and with each part necessary to the well-being and success of the whole. The doctrine which pertains to the collective of Christians, or the Body of Christ, is a very important teaching in Scripture. Unfortunately, the non-Christian world's emphasis on individual advancement has infiltrated our belief system and the Church is missing the application of these valuable truths.

Ballet has given me an understanding and appreciation of how the Body of Christ is supposed to function. As a dancer, I am aware of the necessity of bringing every single part of the body, from the foot to the eye, into unity and harmony in subjection to the head. A beautiful dance is created when all the pieces and parts work together as one.

While dancing professionally, I was plagued by a very painful little toe, which would swell to twice its size before any major performance. But for the love of dance, I pushed through the pain. To compensate for the pain, I walked with a limp, favoring that little toe. The limp caused my back to hurt; the back pain brought on a headache; and the headache made me mean. You would not think that such a seemingly insignificant thing as a little toe could cause total dysfunction in my body, but it did. In the same way, if we do not function as we should in the Body of Christ, the Church will not work as God intended. Christ's Body will be handicapped and the world will be deprived of the testimony of God's Church.

Scripture tells us that that as each Christian fulfills his or her responsibility in the Body, lovingly coordinating with each other, the Church will be strengthened and will grow. *"From him (Christ, the Head of the Body) the whole body, joined and held together by every supporting ligament, grows and builds itself up in love, as each part does its work"* *(Ephesians 4:16).*

Each of us was created with our own combination of natural abilities and talents. Our courses in life also give us particular skills, training, and experience. In addition, the Holy Spirit sovereignly distributes to each Christian gifts designed to be used in the building up of the Body. No two of us are alike; all are special and unique blends of these natural and spiritual gifts. The Church will only function as it was intended when each believer takes the place in the Body for which he or she was particularly designed.

Sometimes God takes our natural abilities and talents and anoints them for His service. When I married Frank, I thought that would be the end of my dancing. Who ever heard of a dancing preacher's wife? But I never ceased expressing my love for the Father through dance. My heart danced within me when I praised Him and in the privacy of my home I danced to Christian music. I sacrificed something I loved very much, never dreaming that God would one day give it back to me for His glory and the furtherance of the Kingdom.

Early in my marriage with small children and my obligations at Briarwood, it seemed like I was in a little Christian cocoon. I wanted desperately to find a way to reach women for Christ apart from the church. Also, about that time Anita and Peggy, aged three and five, expressed an interest in taking ballet. Of course we could not afford the lessons, but I told them we would ask God to provide a way. An opportunity came one day when I ran into the director of the ballet school associated with the company I had previously danced with. She asked me if I was still dancing and I told her no, that I was a preacher's wife.

"A preacher's wife!" She was shocked.

As our conversation went on, she asked me to teach some classes for her on a part-time basis. My immediate response was no, preachers' wives do not dance. Seeing that this could be an answer to my prayers for contact outside the church and an opportunity for my girls to take ballet in a premier school, I prayed and found nothing in the Bible that prohibited it.

I summoned my courage and asked Frank what he thought. He said he would pray about it and then talk to the Session of the church, because he thought God might be opening a door to use me in the ballet school. Most of the elders were fairly new Christians and had not been raised with the legalism which taught that dancing was a "sin." They said they saw no difference between teaching tennis lessons and teaching ballet and agreed that I should take the opportunity.

My little girls enrolled in the ballet school, but more importantly, they saw God answer their prayer. But even better, I had the privilege to reach out to non-Christians and share the Gospel, not as a preacher's wife, but as a ballet teacher. It was a win-win situation all the way around and God was glorified. Six weeks after I started teaching, the ballet director became a Christian.

As the years went by, teaching at the school became more and more demanding and I longed to see ballet itself used as a ministry tool. Also, as a paid teacher for the school, I did not have the freedom to invite people who could not pay to take classes. So I began to pray for God to open a door. One day the church administrator at Briarwood came and asked me to teach ballet at the church after school. He said we offered all kinds of sports activities, why not ballet.

That first year there were 40 students, the second year, 70, and by the third year we were up to 120. Currently over 500 students are enrolled at the Briarwood campus. We have a performing company, the Ballet Exaltation, which is used for various ministry opportunities in schools, churches, and conferences across the United States. In addition, the Ballet Exaltation has traveled overseas opening new doors for mission organizations in those countries. In distinctively unique ways, God has provided a faculty of very qualified, Godly ballet instructors who believe in the mission focus of the school. Our mission statement expresses our vision to use dance as a tool for evangelizing, discipling, and worship, responding to the reformed mandate to bring the arts into the service of the Lord Jesus Christ.

Years before, I gave up a talent and passion that God had given me. He stripped me of my own self-sufficiency and selfish ambitions and, after a while, gave ballet back to me to use for His glory and the building up of the Body of Christ. How good is our God!

In addition to the natural gift of dance, God has given me the spiritual gift of hospitality. It is obvious that it came from God because it definitely did not come naturally. When I married Frank, nothing in my previous life prepared me for God's calling in this area. But in Frank's eyes, my inadequacy was just another opportunity to trust God. He never wavered in his determination to use our home as a conduit for ministry. Therefore, I had no choice but to give God my fears, jump right in, and leave the results in His hands. He has always been faithful, but it took me years to feel comfortable in exercising this gift.

The Saturday after we returned from our honeymoon, Frank asked a few friends to come for dessert following the Sunday evening service. I made a supposedly no-fail Betty Crocker cake for my debut as the pastor's wife. For me it was a huge step. That night as he was cutting the cake, the knife literally would not go through. I am sure I followed the directions correctly, but the cake was like a cement block! Horrified, I watched two of the men toss the cake like a football, laughing their heads off. Looking back now, it might seem funny, but at the time I was devastated.

Many of the spiritual gifts God bestows are not obvious and others may not appreciate them. But God has a plan and knows what He is doing. The following verses in I Corinthians 12 tell us that we should accept our gifts and roles in the Body because God gives them as He pleases. We should not wish that we had different ones. Also, we should not view the "less desirable" gifts as "less valuable." *"On the contrary, those parts of the Body that seem to be weaker are indispensable, and the parts that we think are less honorable we treat with special honor. And the parts that are unpresentable are treated with special modesty, while our presentable parts need no special treatment. But God has combined the members of the Body and has given greater honor to the parts that lacked it, so that there should be no division in the Body, but that its parts should have equal concern for each other. If one part suffers, every part suffers with it; if one part is honored, every part rejoices with it" (I Corinthians 12:22-26).*

Each spring our ballet school at Briarwood performs an allegorical story ballet that shares the Gospel. The students know that each one of them is crucial in the performance. I tell the little girls, "You may be just a butterfly, but your part is very important in setting the stage to tell the story." Therefore, they learn that they must do their part well in order for the message to be told.

If you do not take the place which God assigns and for which He equips you, the Body suffers. Not only will you miss the blessing of being God's instrument, but the effectiveness of the whole Church will be compromised. Nothing can thwart the purposes of God, but the consequences of failing to function in the place which God has given results in the loss of the privilege and joy of ministry. For years, our house was the central location for the youth group. After one of their functions, I found cheese crackers crushed into the carpet. With disgust I told Frank, "Those kids don't care anything about our house. They take us for granted." I continued my rampage as I cleaned up. After a while, Frank looked at me and said, "Barbara, if you complain about the cost of ministry, God will remove the privilege of ministry." That one simple statement changed my attitude toward the opportunities God brings to serve Him. Almost every day now, I see the fruit of that ministry. Those "careless kids" have grown up to be elders, teachers, mothers, businessmen, missionaries, and preachers.

*Frank Barker: "Barbara, if you
complain about the cost of the ministry,
God will remove the privilege of ministry."*

What is the purpose of the Body? Let me begin by telling you what its purpose is not. The Church does not exist for the glorification and exaltation of individuals. It exists for God's own glory. Once while on my way to an important speaking engagement in North Carolina, I drove through the mountains, preoccupied with the thoughts of how I would be perceived. The following night I had a dream that I was driving through those same mountains seeing the signs along the way, "Scenic View – Two Miles," "Scenic View – One Mile," and "Scenic View – ½ Mile." Finally I came to an overlook with a spectacular display of God's glorious creation. A sign on the other side of the road featured a big arrow pointing to this magnificent vista. In my dream I was standing with my back to the view gazing up at the sign. I suddenly awakened and God seemed to be saying, "Barbara, that's what's wrong with you. You want to be the sign everybody looks at. The truth is that the only purpose of the sign is to direct people's vision to the glory of God."

In our "me-oriented" society, people have a tendency to think the purpose of the Church is to meet their personal needs, or should I say "wants." They complain when the music does not make them feel "worshipful" or when there are not enough workers in the nursery. And heaven forbid if the pastor preaches too long and they do not beat the Baptists to the Cracker Barrel. People hop from church to church looking for a place where they are happy and "feel at home" without taking time to ask God where He wants to use them.

Our emphasis should not be about what we **get** from Church, but what we **give.** Scripture does not support a motive of self-advancement in our service; even though, the product of our service will have its personal rewards. Ephesians 4:12-13 tells us that the Church exists *"to prepare God's people for works of service, so that the body of Christ may be built up until we all reach unity in the faith and in the knowledge of the Son of God and become mature, attaining to the whole measure of the fullness of Christ."* The Bible is very clear about how the Body should function. Each member, practicing humility, meekness, and deference to one another, submits to Christ as the head. The result is an effective and efficient working of the Body of Christ. As we each do our part, we participate in the sanctification process of other believers; God is glorified; and the lost are drawn to Christ. Blessings come to individuals as a by-product of their service to others.

God draws the Body of Christ together for His own glory and for the mutual edification of its members. My responsibility within it is to minister and receive the ministry of others. As I have put into practice these principles in my own life, giving to God by serving others in the Church, I have personally received far more than I ever gave. I am overwhelmed to think of how God has used other Christians to encourage me by rebuking, serving, loving, and confronting me. In the beginning God Himself said, *"It is not good for the man to be alone" (Genesis 2:18).* I need the Body of Christ and so do you.

I especially need their prayers. Doctors have commented to me that they do not understand how I can function with the deteriorated condition of my back. I always tell them that it is because the people at Briarwood pray for me. Along with their prayers, I need their fellowship in my loneliness, their strength in my weakness, and their admonition when I stray in thoughts and actions.

Sometimes pride and self-sufficiency keep us from confessing our need for the ministry of others. A young man came to Frank one time and told him he was leaving the church. He went on to say that he desired to get married and had asked every eligible, single woman at Briarwood out for a date and none would go. Frank asked him to commit to stay for six more months while they prayed fervently for God to bring him a wife. Frank also said he would ask all the prayer groups and Bible studies he was involved in to join in the prayer. Sure enough, before the six months ended God brought the perfect woman for him and she later became his wife. God used the Body of Christ greatly in that man's life after he humbly came forward with his need.

God requires that we should be faithful stewards of the gifts and resources He has entrusted to us. *"Now it is required that those who have been given a trust must prove faithful" (I Corinthians 4:2).* Stewardship is using what He has given in such a way that we give it back to Him. Dr. E. V. Hill, a pastor from Watts, Los Angeles, said, "God will give it to you if He can get it through you."

On that day when we see Him face to face, God Himself will hold us accountable for our steward-ship of all that He has given us. This accountability is particularly true concerning the resources, both physical and spiritual, He has bestowed for the building up of His Body and the furtherance of His Kingdom.

> *E. V. Hill: "God will give it to you*
> *If He can get it through you."*

STEWARDSHIP

*S*hepherd of Israel – Thank You for shepherding me with Your rod and Your staff. Use me to shepherd others.

*T*eacher of Truth – Thank You for not leaving me in darkness. Use me to teach others.

*E*quipper of the saints – Thank You for the privilege of ministering in Your Church. May I faithfully use Your gifts.

*W*arrior of God – Thank You for the victory You have won in which I stand. May I be faithful in the fight of faith.

*A*uthor of my faith – Thank You for opening my eyes and my heart and calling me to Yourself. Use me to open eyes.

*R*ewarder of faithfulness – Thank You for Your discipline of sowing and reaping. May I be a sower in Your vineyard.

*D*estroyer of Death – Thank You for having opened the door to heaven and to eternal life!! May I point others to You.

*S*avior of the world – Thank You for the love that brought You to the cross to redeem me from the wages of my sin.

*H*elper of the Helpless – Thank You for Your constant provision of strength in my weakness. May I strengthen others.

*I*ntercessor for the saints – Thank You for standing at God's right hand to pray for me and to keep me. Make me an intercessor.

*P*lease, Lord Jesus – in light of all You have done for me, make me a good steward of Your blessings and gifts.[1]

MY PRAYER

Dear Lord, I am so thankful that you gave me gifts, abilities, and talents to be used to serve my brothers and sisters in Christ. I pray you would give me opportunities to serve and I would have the right attitude and motivation – all for Your glory and the furtherance of Your kingdom. Amen.

Notes

[1] Barker, Barbara B.

Chapter 7
PERSONAL APPLICATION

1. In the past, how have you been more of a "taker" than a "giver" in your Church?

2. What gifts, abilities, or talents are you not currently utilizing? Why not?

3. Is there a gift you are not currently utilizing that you would like to have the opportunity to use?

4. What are you going to do differently as a result of this study?

Chapter 7
BIBLE STUDY

What do you learn about the Body of Christ from the following verses?
- Romans 12:5
- I Corinthians 12:27
- Ephesians 1:22-23
- Ephesians 4:11-13
- Colossians 2:19

Those verses are packed full of great truths. I don't want you to miss one of them. In which of the above verses did you learn that:
- Individually, Christians have many forms but only one Body?
- God causes the Body to grow?
- Christians make up the Body of Christ?
- Christ is the Head of the Body?
- Spiritual gifts prepare God's people for service so that the Body is built up?
- Members of the Body belong to one another?
- Each member has his/her own part or function?
- Christ fills the Body in every way?
- As the Body is built up, it becomes mature and the members are unified?

God gives each Christian at least one spiritual gift. What are some of those gifts mentioned in the following verses: Romans 12:6-8; I Corinthians 12:8-10, 28-30; Ephesians 4:11?

Read I Corinthians 12:12-26. In the light of this passage, how do you view your role in the Church? How do you view the role of other believers?

Notice that the "Love Chapter" follows in I Corinthians 13. What part does love play in the exercising of spiritual gifts (I Corinthians 12:31)?

The Bible uses other metaphors to describe the Church. What are those metaphors and what additional insight do you gain from them?
- II Corinthians 11:2, Revelation 19:7
- John 1:12; Romans 8:15, 9:26; II Corinthians 6:18
- Luke 12:32; John 10:14-16
- Matthew 25:34, James 2:5
- Ephesians 2:19
- Ephesians 2:20-22; I Corinthians 3:9
- I Corinthians 3:16-17
- I Peter 2:4,5,9
- II Corinthians 6:16; I Corinthians 6:19

Read the Parable of the Talents in Matthew 25:14-28. What lessons do you learn from this passage?

Chapter 7
DISCUSSION QUESTIONS

1. How has this study changed the way you view your role in the Body of Christ?

2. What are your natural gifts and abilities? How have you used them in the Body of Christ?

3. What is your spiritual gift (or gifts)?

4. How are you exercising them in the Body?

5. What results have you seen?

6. What part does the Holy Spirit play in the utilization of gifts, talents, and abilities?

7. What happens when someone volunteers for a job that is outside his/her gift mix?

CHAPTER 8

God's Design for Submission

*Tim Townes, Barbara's son-in-law who
is married to Peggy:
"If women understood the Barker women's
definition of submission, they wouldn't have
a problem with it."*

Submission is considered a politically incorrect word in our society today, often associated with being subservient and assuming an inferior role. This is not at all what the Bible teaches. One's value does not come from his or her role in life. Value comes from being made in the image of God, a creation of the great Creator. Submission for a Christian is a good thing and a way to express love for God.

The Christian life is about worship, which is focusing on the character of God and letting that experience overflow into actions and attitudes. If you think about it, submitting is a form of worship. Submission is first and foremost about yielding ourselves to God's control. The attitude of submission overflows out of a worship of God's omniscience, sovereignty, and love.

Jesus is our ultimate example in everything, and He was no stranger to submission. We see that in His very act of becoming man, He submitted to the will of His Father: *"(Jesus), who, being in very nature God, did not consider equality with God something to be grasped, but made himself nothing, taking the very nature of a servant, being made in human likeness. And being found in appearance as a man, he humbled himself and became obedient to death — even death on a cross!" (Philippians 2:6-8).* If Christ Himself, Who was God, submitted Himself to His Father, who are we to do less?

To whom should we submit? The Bible instructs all of us to submit to God (James 4:7), leaders (Hebrews 13:17), earthly governing authorities (I Peter 2:13-14), and to one another (Ephesians 5:21). Children should submit to parents (Ephesians 6:1), wives to husbands (Ephesians 5:22), and employees to their employers (Ephesians 6:5). Because we are created for relationship, no one is exempt from submission.

What is God's purpose in having us submit to an authority? There are basically three reasons: to bring unity, peace, and order to relationships; to provide protection to the one under submission; and even more importantly, submission in earthly relationships gives us practice in submitting to God.

God loves us very much and before the beginning of time established a good and perfect plan for our lives. As we submit our wills to His, we become beneficiaries of His abundance. Just like muscles become stronger with exercise, the act of surrendering our own desires and agendas becomes easier with practice. That is a principle reason we teach our children to obey us. Children who obey their earthly parents find it easier to obey their Heavenly Father.

In every structured relationship, whether it is the church, marriage, family, work, or government, there must be one person who has the "final say." If this were not the case, chaos would result from perpetual power struggles. After all, every one of us thinks our opinion is the right one. If not, we would not have it.

God has also ordained the structure of submission within relationships for our own protection. All authorities are ordained by God and He will use them as His instruments to direct, provide for, protect, and even chasten those under their care. These authorities are like God's sheltering umbrellas. Anyone who chooses to operate outside established shelters becomes vulnerable to harmful consequences – just like a child who wanders outside a protective playground fence.

Who is the one that benefits within an authority/submission relationship? When the Biblical guidelines for relationships are followed, the answer is most definitely the one under authority. Scripture teaches and Jesus modeled a servant-hearted, love-based leadership style. Christ so loved the Church that He sacrificially gave His life for her. A husband is instructed to love his wife (Ephesians 5:25), care for her (Ephesians 5:29), encourage her spiritual growth (Ephesians 5:26), not to be harsh with her (Colossians 3:19), and to be considerate and respectful (I Peter 3:7).

Those in authority roles should take their responsibility very seriously. Scripture teaches that they will be judged more severely. *"Not many of you should presume to be teachers, my brothers, because you know that we who teach will be judged more strictly" (James 3:1). "And if anyone causes one of these little ones who believes in me to sin, it would be better for him to be thrown into the sea with a large millstone tied around his neck" (Mark 9:42).*

When Frank and I were dating, I listened to him and his friends talk about their flying adventures and became fascinated with the idea of soaring the skies rising above the pull of gravity. While going to college in Chicago, a friend who owned a plane invited me to go flying with him. After my first flight I was in love, with flying that is. He let me take the controls sometimes when we flew and later on I used his plane to take lessons. So eventually, I became a pilot.

The mechanics of how a plane flew were Greek to me. I passed the multiple-choice flight exams by deductive logic. When it came to examining the plane during the pre-flight inspection, I just went around looking and nodding like I saw the instructor do. I had no clue what I was looking for.

Several years later after Frank and I broke up, I noticed a plane for sale just like the one I flew in Chicago. I knew I had to have it. The price happened to be the exact amount of the value of the stock that my daddy gave me when I graduated from college.

The only problem was that my daddy was dead set against my buying it. Also, our family's insurance man would not sell me damage insurance, only liability, because of his misgivings about that particular plane. There were many sign posts that alerted me to the dangers in what I was determined to do, but I ignored them all. The biggest red flag, which I also ignored, appeared when I did the pre-flight inspection on the plane. The engine was really oily, very different from the whistle clean plane I had flown before. When I asked the owner about it, he said he would clean it up. There were also unusual little trim tabs on the wings, which he said were to help fight torque on takeoff. I did not know enough to question his explanation.

The stock certificates which I planned to use to purchase the plane were in a bank in Houston and Jack Valenti was the co-signer on the account. (Yes, this is the same Jack Valenti who was head of the Motion Picture Association of America and one of the most influential men in the entertainment industry.) I had worked for Jack in Houston, and we had dated some. Anyway, the big challenge in buying the plane was that I needed the money by noon on Friday – there was another interested buyer, or so I was told. It would be a miracle if Jack would be in town and could get the money to me in time. Ignoring all of the warning signs, I let that be my fleece. I thought, why should I listen to my daddy, he was not even a Christian at the time. If only I had followed God's principles of submission, I could have prevented the disaster that was to come.

Sure enough, everything worked like clockwork and the stock certificates made it to Birmingham right at the last minute. I walked into the lawyer's office at 20 minutes before noon and bought the plane.

It did not take long to realize that I had made a **big** mistake. My sister's husband went out to the airport to fly the plane and everyone there told him I had bought a lemon. It turned out that the previous owner had lied to me and given me incorrect flight records. He had said there were 200 hours left before it needed a major overhaul, but in reality, the plane was 300 hours past. Because he had not paid for the re-fabrication of the wings, there was a lien on the plane, which meant I could not fly it out of the Birmingham airport. It soon became very apparent that I had stepped outside of God's will and messed up royally.

So I decided to "sanctify" the plane by lending it to Southeastern Bible College to train pilots who were preparing for the mission field. But more importantly, I asked God and my daddy to forgive me for going outside God's established authority structure.

Just when I thought it could not get any worse, my brother-in-law wrecked the plane. While taking off, the engine threw a rod, causing the plane to dive 40 feet, nose first. Fortunately, he walked away unscathed. But the accident demolished the propeller, engine, and nose gear. The cockpit was ruined by the oil that poured in during the descent. The plane was totaled, and I came to the sad realization that I deserved nothing better. God had clearly shown me, through my father, not to buy the plane, but I ignored all the rules of guidance. Without damage insurance, I had nothing left of my money or the plane.

A short time later I got a wire from the Wright Patterson Air Force Base Flying Club in Ohio. They asked me what I wanted for the wrecked airplane. I wrote back and told them it was a glider (without an engine), the nose gear and propeller were crushed, and the cockpit was ruined. Surprisingly, they wired me a $400 check and told me to hold it until they could get there and another $1,000 would be paid when they took possession. The next week they flew in a mechanic with the spare parts, who started working on the plane. After a day and a half, it was ready to fly. My brother-in-law straightened out the lien issue with the lawyer who represented me in the sale and the Flying Club took possession. Selling that little wrecked plane was a miracle and an example of God's mercy and goodness, which I clearly did not deserve.

Interestingly enough, in the meantime, the value of my stock had dropped, so I could buy back nearly all that I had sold. In this particular case, once I acknowledged my sin and made recompense, God in His mercy restored my loss. But more importantly, He left me with a new appreciation of His purpose for submission.

More than anything, I want to be quick to obey God when He directs. In order to learn to obey Him quickly, I must first learn how to obey my earthly authorities quickly – even when we do not agree.

Now that does not mean I will quit voicing my opinions and become everyone's doormat. Scripture does not support that view of submission. Josh McDowell, Christian author and speaker, has said that true submission is voicing your opinion and, once your authority has gone against your opinion, supporting him/her 100% without voicing your opinion again. In no way should those in submissive roles minimize the importance of their influence on authorities. Many times God directs and leads authorities through those who are submissive to them.

I must interject here that if an authority requires that you do something which is clearly prohibited in Scripture, you must first and foremost follow Scripture. Examples include a boss who requires employees to lie or falsify records, a parent that asks a child to steal, or a husband who demands a wife commit prostitution. These are extreme examples, which are obviously against the laws of God and laws of man.

Submission sometimes requires developing creative alternatives to an authority's directives. Take Daniel of the Old Testament as an example. When he and his buddies were taken as slaves to Babylon, they were required to eat foods which were forbidden by the Law. Instead of butting heads with their guard, they presented an alternative which would require God's intervention. They proposed that instead of eating the rich food and wine from the king's table, they would eat vegetables and water for ten days, confident they would do as well as the other young men. Sure enough, Daniel and company were healthier and better nourished. Everybody won and God got the glory (Daniel 1). Daniel was very wise to discern that the food was not their keepers' objective, but their health. He correctly surmised that an alternative means, with God's help, could still result in the same desired end result. The creative alternative turned out to be a win-win for everyone. The guard's authority remained in tact, Daniel and his friends were healthy specimens for the king, and God's Law was honored.

In conclusion, submission begins with a teachable heart toward the Lord, confident that His plan for our lives is best. Next we must be assured that He is in control of every earthly authority relationship and will work through given authority structures for His eternal purposes. Finally, and probably the most difficult, we must die to our own desires in order to advance God's Kingdom.

MY PRAYER

Dear Lord, deep down I know Your ways are always best. But I confess that many times I want my own way and rebel against the authority structures You have ordained in my life. Please help me see the authorities as Your instruments who carry out Your plans. I want to submit to them as unto You. I pray this in the Name of the ultimate example of submission, Jesus. Amen.

Chapter 8
PERSONAL APPLICATION

1. Who are the "authorities" in your life and what is your attitude toward each of them (e.g. husband, parents, teachers, employers, etc)?

2. Is there an area in which you are rebelling against an authority, either in action or attitude?

3. How does changing your attitude affect your actions?

Chapter 8
BIBLE STUDY

Ultimately, to whom are you responsible?

Who is in control of everything that affects your life?

Does this Person love you and care about what happens to you?

God, in His perfection, designed accountability and order in relationships. According to the following verses, who should submit and to what authority?

- James 4:7
- Hebrews 13:7
- I Peter 2:13-14, Romans 13:1
  additional: why do you submit?
- I Peter 5:5
- Ephesians 6:1
- Ephesians 5:22, I Peter 3:1
- Ephesians 6:5
  (what's the modern day application of this verse?)
- Ephesians 5:21
  additional: why do you submit?

Ultimately, we don't want to submit because we want our own way. What do the following verses say about getting our own way?

- Luke 14:33
- Romans 13:14
- I Peter 4:2
- I Corinthians 10:24

So when we resist our authority, Who are we really resisting?

What promise can we claim (I Peter 5:6)?

Chapter 8
DISCUSSION QUESTIONS

1. Before this chapter, what was you view of submission?

2. Has this study changed your view? If so, how?

3. Have you ever had to submit to an authority you did not respect? How did God bring good out of that situation?

4. In what relationships are you the authority? How has (or will) this study affected your attitudes and actions toward those in your care?

5. What does one's role have to do with one's value or worth? How does your answer affect your desire to submit?

CHAPTER 9

Only God Can Change a Person

Our oldest daughter, Anita, was an intelligent child and memorized the Catechism easily at a young age. When she was just a little girl, I would get her up in front of groups and ask her, "Who made you?"

She would say, "God."

"What else did God make?"

"God made all things."

"Why did God make all things?"

"For His own glory." On and on through the Catechism we would go. I wanted everyone to be as impressed as I was with her intelligence (and with me as her mother).

One day at a friend's house, I started asking Anita the Catechism questions in front of the other moms who were gathered there. All of a sudden she stopped. I could tell by looking at her face that at that very moment she realized her mother was showing her off like a trained seal. She refused to answer any more of the questions. And from that point on she bristled every time she sensed my exploiting her for my own benefit. Needless to say, this was an underlying barrier in our relationship until she went to college. On the outside, it looked like we had a good relationship, but there was not the closeness that comes from being truly open with one another.

I regret the years of emotional distance. But by God's grace, Anita and I resolved those past issues. After she went to college, we sat down and talked about everything. She told me she always thought she had to perform for me, which she resented. I admitted that I wanted to show her off and use her for my "reputation" and asked for her forgiveness. With a lot of tears, prayer, and constructive planning, we worked through the breakdowns in our relationship. Part of the solution was a commitment to pray together every week and make ourselves really talk to each other. Over time we have grown close and God has restored to us the years that the locusts of anger, resentment, and pride had eaten (Joel 2:25). Even though she lives in Arizona, is a mom of four active children, and a preacher's wife, we have a very special relationship today.

One of the most frustrating things in the world for a parent, teacher, discipler, pastor, friend, etc. is to realize that no one can truly change another person or mold them into a desired image. You can certainly be an agent for change, that is, an instrument God uses in another's life to bring about a change of heart or behavior. But the key to being an effective change agent is to pray without ceasing and depend on God to deal with their hearts as He guides your words and actions. And then, the hardest part is to leave the results to Him.

The goal of the parent, teacher, discipler, etc. should be to see God so work in the heart and character of a person that he or she automatically responds to God's law for the purpose of pleasing Him. Sometimes you can affect behavior temporarily through rewards, punishments, and expectations, but only God can permanently change a heart.

One time I was speaking at Montreat conference center along with Mrs. Billy Graham. My children were little, ages four, five, and six. All the way to Asheville, North Carolina I preached to them, "You have to be good. Everybody will be looking at you because I am the speaker." I laid this huge burden on them, as if my credibility as a Bible teacher depended on their good behavior.

The one thing I remember from that conference is Mrs. Graham's saying, "We never teach our children to perform for the benefit of our reputation. Instead we teach them that they have only One to please and that is God Himself. When they learn that it is God Who knows their hearts and thoughts and He is the One they're seeking to please, then their lives will be directed toward Him. We need not worry about the rest." I went immediately and gathered up my children and told them they were to be good for the Lord, not for me. That was a pivotal moment when I realized my responsibility as a mother is to mold them from the inside out, not from the outside in.

Another learning moment was when I went to hear a missionary speak in the chapel program at Briarwood Christian School and sat behind some rowdy kids. After it was over, I rebuked them for their behavior, telling them that since they went to a Christian school, they should **act** like Christians. As I walked out, it was like the Holy Spirit asked me, "Is that what we are teaching them, that they should '**act** like a Christian'?" I realized that a Christian's behavior is not an act or a performance. Christ-like actions should be a result of His working in them. Their behavior should be an overflow of what God was doing in their hearts, not a "put-on." Therefore, I like to define the Christian life based on Philippians 1:11 and John 15:4 in this way: "The Christian life is the out-flowing of the indwelling life of Christ."

> **The Christian life is the out-flowing of the indwelling life of Christ.**

Now, this does not mean that a person in authority should not demand certain standards of behavior. However, it should be made clear that the requirement for such behavior is to meet the standards of that person or organization. For instance, a business may require a certain dress code. For an employee to accept employment at that business, the requirement should be adhered to. However, he has the choice as to whether or not he will work in that place. When a parent forbids a child to listen to certain kinds of music, the child must realize that obedience and submission is part of living under the authority of his parents. The child must trust God to guide his parents for his own good.

Just because a certain behavior is prohibited in a given situation does not mean that it is **always** wrong. In another situation and under a different authority, there may be freedom for that behavior. Only what God clearly identifies in Scripture as sin (the breaking of God's Law) should be prohibited.

Imposing your standards on another can lead to legalism, if not handled carefully. Legalism is defined as imposing your own "interpretation of spirituality" on another person for the purpose of having him meet your expectations. It is focusing on the outward conformity of a person without concern for the heart. To declare a thing sin when it is not declared sin in Scripture is legalism – a serious danger for a Christian.

> ***Legalism . . . is focusing on the outward conformity of a person without concern for the heart.***

My sister, Anita, is a very godly woman; however, when she first became a Christian she was nurtured under very legalistic teaching. She cried and cried over the fact that I was going to hell because I was a ballet dancer. Needless to say, I was turned off by her. Before I became a Christian, I was a student at Northwestern University in Chicago and often visited friends at a Bible college nearby. I noticed that the girls did not wear lipstick and their dress seemed rather austere. When I mentioned I was a ballet dancer, I sensed their disapproval. For me, before becoming a Christian, legalism became synonymous with Christianity. It was not until I understood the biblical definition of sin and came to know Christ personally that my opinion changed. Incidentally, when my dear sister led me to Christ, she had already come into the freedom of knowing God and the joy of serving Him out of thankfulness rather than obligation.

There are standards of behavior that are more appropriate in given situations. That does not mean that non-conformity to those standards is necessarily a sin. Drinking alcohol is a prime example.

When Frank went to seminary, he quit drinking. Soon after that, he attended a wedding of a Navy buddy. At the reception all the guys gathered around the trunk of a car and passed a bottle. It came around to Frank and, not wanting to make a big deal about it, he took a swig and passed it on. Most of them did not even know he was in seminary. Later on that night, one of the inebriated guys' wife was trying to get him to stop drinking. Frank overheard the man's justifying his behavior by saying, "The preacher's drinking." Right then and there Frank committed that alcohol would never again pass his lips. Frank, more than anyone I have ever met, desires to be used by God to draw others to Himself and knows his actions can make a powerful statement for the Gospel. In the Bible Belt drinking often causes one's Christian testimony to be called into question. Although the Bible does not say that drinking in and of itself is a sin,

Frank purposed that his actions would never be used as justification for a weaker brother in that area.

Another area of legalism with which I am most familiar is dancing. John Frame, a professor at Westminster Seminary in California, was at one time considered the authority of reformed worship. One Saturday I went to the church for ballet rehearsals and noticed there was a PCA (Presbyterian Church in America) conference on music and worship being held in the sanctuary. As I walked in the door, I caught snippets of conversations from the groups of people gathered around the foyer. I asked someone what was going on and he told me that Dr. Frame's message the night before compared modern-day reformed worship with legitimate Biblical worship. Dr. Frame said he would not be offended at all if a preacher called the people to dance in the aisles, but rehearsed art forms such as ballet would not be acceptable. He also condemned ballet because of its association with an avant-garde lifestyle and the dancers' immodest attire. At the time everyone's mouths dropped because obviously he was not aware of Briarwood's ballet ministry.

I went to Dr. Frame and asked him to visit our rehearsal. During a break in the conference, he came and watched the girls' practice at the barre, clearly impressed with the amount of work and skill involved. For a recent PCA Women's conference in Atlanta, we had performed a long piece entitled "The Glory of the Resurrection," which interlaced Scripture with Christian music, both classical as well as contempo-rary. I invited him to come back later and watch the girls perform the piece in their costumes. Graciously he accepted.

When he arrived there was a whole entourage of people with him who wanted to know his reaction. The girls danced beautifully with radiant faces reflecting their worship of the Lord. I watched Dr. Frame's reaction out of the corner of my eye and saw that his eyes were welling with tears; he was watching with an engaged expression, not one of judgment.

After it was over, he was very quiet for a moment and then said, "I spoke of what I did not know. I have never seen anything like this. It is indeed worship."

With all humility I asked, "Isn't the reformed mandate that we bring all of the arts back into the service of the Lord and use them for His glory?"

He smiled and said yes.

I continued, "Isn't the choir a rehearsed art form?"

He chuckled and said yes.

"Don't you think that God could redeem dance and use it for His glory."

He said, "Yes, I do . . . now."

I went on to ask him a series of questions, not trying to put him on the spot, but sincerely wanting to know his perspective. He was very gracious in his responses. After he left Birmingham, he wrote Frank saying that he was grateful for being introduced to a blessing he had not known. Later on he included this experience in a book on worship.

Sometimes our "legalistic" views are formed when we are not fully informed, or when we are limited in our understanding. That is why it is so important that all of our opinions be based on Scripture.

**Sometimes our "legalistic" views
are formed when we are not fully informed,
or when we are limited in our understanding.**

If I cannot "guilt" another person to "act right," how do I influence them? First, I make sure that my motivations are pure and that their changing is for the glory of God and not for my own purposes. Sometimes in Bible teaching situations, the teacher's primary goal is to have her students become dependent on her. Quite a few of the people Frank led to the Lord and discipled ended up going to other churches. I became offended by what I perceived as their ingratitude, but he would just say, "Honey, God called us to build His Kingdom. He will take care of Briarwood." It is hard to keep that in mind. The truth is my role should be to build up Christians and then turn them over to God for Him to use anywhere and in any capacity that He sees fit. After all, that is exactly what we desire for our children: they would be independently dependent on God, not us, and would live out His plan, not ours, for their lives.

Secondly, I must acknowledge that prayer is the most effective tool I have for affecting another's spiritual growth. Colossians 1:9 tells us: *"For this reason, since the day we heard about you, we have not stopped praying for you and asking God to fill you with the knowledge of his will through all spiritual wisdom and understanding."* I Samuel 12:23-24 says, *"As for me, far be it from me that I should sin against the LORD by failing to pray for you. And I will teach you the way that is good and right. But be sure to fear the LORD and serve him faithfully with all your heart; consider what great things he has done for you."*

I pray for my children and grandchildren constantly, that they would have thankful hearts and never cease to appreciate the grace and goodness of God. I want them to walk in such a way that God will be pleased. I do not pray for easy lives for them, but that they would be more than conquerors in difficult places. My prayers focus on their developing the character of Christ, not experiencing the comforts of life.

> *My prayers focus on their developing*
> *the character of Christ,*
> *not experiencing the comforts of life.*

Sometimes it is appropriate to ask God to strip your loved ones of all that forms a barrier to Him. Hold on tight and do not resist when God takes them through the hard times because He will use the difficulties to conform them to Himself. A prime example of this is a young man who was in Briarwood's youth group many years ago. He was not a Christian and I had prayed for him for years. I ran into him one day when he was in college and he said to me, "I don't owe God anything. I have my own money and my own car and I'm working my own way through college."

I said, "Oh, Tommy, I'm going to pray for you because everything you have could be taken away in a heartbeat. What you really need is God."

He just scowled. A few weeks later he called in the middle of the night. "Mrs. Barker, quit praying for me." It turns out that after our talk he had gotten sick and could not go to class or work. He was not able to pay his bills and someone ran into his car. God got his attention and he eventually surrendered to Him. After college he came on staff at Briarwood, finished seminary, and served as the Administrative Pastor for many years.

Thirdly, I realize my sincere love and concern for someone can be a powerfully effective change agent in a person's life. It has been said that someone will not care what you know, until he knows that you care. Paul says in I Thessalonians 2, verses seven and eight, *"As apostles of Christ we could have been a burden to you, but we were gentle among you, like a mother caring for her little children. We loved you so much that we were delighted to share with you not only the gospel of God but our lives as well, because you had become so dear to us."* Paul was a bold witness for Christ, but he also loved his flock dearly.

Fourthly, communicating Truth is a necessary part of seeing a person change, even when the Truth hurts. If someone is driving down a road and you know the bridge is out ahead, you have to warn him. In the same way, if a person is participating in a harmful behavior, you have to point out the error, even if you risk alienating them.

Lastly, modeling a Godly life results in changed lives. So much of my own Christian walk is the direct result of Frank's living out the Spirit-filled life before me. I ultimately embraced radical faith because I saw it working in his life. He told me many times, "Barbara, God will never do it **through** us unless He does it **in** us. We can never tell someone to trust God unless we are trusting Him ourselves." It has been said, "People are not as interested in our relationship with Christ as in our resemblance to Him."

> *"People are not as interested*
> *in our relationship with Christ*
> *as in our resemblance to Him."*

Paul says in Titus 2:7, *"In everything set them an example by doing what is good."* And then in II Thessalonians 3:7-9, *"For you yourselves know how you ought to follow our example. We were not idle when we were with you, nor did we eat anyone's food without paying for it. On the contrary, we worked night and day, laboring and toiling so that we would not be a burden to any of you. We did this, not because we do not have the right to such help, but in order to make ourselves a model for you to follow."*

I do not ever want to be a stumbling block for another person. I check my life constantly and ask the Lord to reveal anything that would cause someone to not trust Christ. I ask myself, "Am I living in such a way that I could urge others to 'follow my example'?" Whether I tell them to imitate me or not, they will. That is a sobering thought. *"So I strive always to keep my conscience clear before God and man" (Acts 24:16).*

MY PRAYER

Dear Lord, I confess that I've tried to change others' behavior by my expectations of them. Teach me how to release them into Your control. I trust You to save them and make them into just the kind of people You would have them to be. Help me to be a loving, prayerful example for them. I also ask that You purify my motivations in loving them. In Christ's name I pray, amen.

Chapter 9
PERSONAL APPLICATION

1. On a scale from 1 to 10, with 1 being totally legalistic and 10 being totally free, where are you? What can you do to experience more freedom?

2. How do you try to influence others?
   - Guilt
   - Expectations
   - Godly example
   - Communicating truth
   - Prayer
   - Other

3. Think of one specific person that you have tried to influence. What were your motives? Were they Christ-like? If not, how would your words and actions change if your motives were right?

Chapter 9
BIBLE STUDY

One of the balances in the Christian life is living between the extremes of legalism and license. Read I Corinthians 10:23-11:1 and paraphrase Paul's explanation of this balance.

Define freedom in Christ according to the following verses:
- Isaiah 61:1
- John 8:32
- Romans 6:16
- Romans 8:2
- Romans 8:21
- II Corinthians 3:17-18
- I Corinthians 8:12
- Galatians 5:13
- I Peter 2:16

According to I Corinthians 3:6-9 and 4:1-5, what does Paul consider his role to be in the lives of the Corinthian Christians? What is his motivation? Who is he trying to please?

What should be your motivation in your relationships with others (I Thessalonians 2:12)?

Relationships provide privileges, but also responsibilities. What is one responsibility according to I Samuel 12:23?

Read the following prayers by Paul and note what he prayed for others.
- Philippians 1:9-11
- Colossians 1:9-12
- Ephesians 1:16-23
- Ephesians 3:14-21

It is also very important to live your life as a reflection of Christ. What do you learn from the following verses?
- Titus 2:7
- II Thessalonians 3:7-9
- Philippians 3:17
- I Timothy 4:12
- I Thessalonians 2:4-12

Chapter 9
DISCUSSION QUESTIONS

1. What are some wrong motivations behind influencing another person?

2. Many times new Christians act very legalistically, but as they mature they do not use "works" to measure spirituality or devotion to God. Discuss this statement. Has this been your observation in others? In yourself?

3. After reading the verses related to freedom in Christ, how would you explain this to another person?

4. What is a Christian free from?

5. Why do some use this freedom as a license to sin? Why is this wrong?

6. How has this study challenged you to pray for others? What specifically will you do differently?

CHAPTER 10

Living above Sin and Weakness

One of the most debilitating teachings of the last decade has been the teaching that I am the "victim" of people and circumstances beyond my control. This philosophy says that I am who I am because of someone else, my situations in life, and the unfairness and inequities to which I have been exposed. My goodness gracious, if one had to have the perfect parents, the perfect school, the perfect job, etc. to be happy and successful, we would be the most pitiful, hopeless, helpless people on earth.

Jesus warns in John 16:33, *"In this world you will have trouble."* He wants us to know that hardships will come in our lives no matter what we do. Some trouble may be by our own hand. When we refuse to acknowledge the authority of God and contrive our own system of morality, we will have trouble and a lot of it. Then there is trouble that comes from living in a fallen world. The "just" part of our nature will cry out when we experience hardships in this way. But Jesus concludes the verse in John 16:33, *"But take heart! I have overcome the world."* That is good news!

The apostle Paul had every opportunity to despair and become discouraged and overcome by hardships. Some of the hardships he endured are outlined in II Corinthians 11:23-28: *"Are they servants of Christ? (I am out of my mind to talk like this.) I am more. I have worked much harder, been in prison more frequently, been flogged more severely, and been exposed to death again and again. Five times I received from the Jews the forty lashes minus one. Three times I was beaten with rods, once I was stoned, three times I was shipwrecked, I spent a night and a day in the open sea, I have been constantly on the move. I have been in danger from rivers, in danger from bandits, in danger from my own countrymen, in danger from Gentiles; in danger in the city, in danger in the country, in danger at sea; and in danger from false brothers. I have labored and toiled and have often gone without sleep; I have known hunger and thirst and have often gone without food; I have been cold and naked. Besides everything else, I face daily the pressure of my concern for all the churches."*

With all of those difficult circumstances, how did Paul continue to rejoice and obey and not succumb to despair, discouragement, or defeat? How could he say toward the end of his life, *"Therefore I will boast all the more gladly about my weaknesses, so that Christ's power may rest on me. That is why, for Christ's sake, I delight in weaknesses, in insults, in*

hardships, in persecutions, in difficulties. For when
I am weak, then I am strong" (II Corinthians 12:9-
10). Simply put, he relied on the promises of God.
"He (God) has given us his very great and precious
promises, so that through them you may participate
in the divine nature and escape the corruption in the
world caused by evil desires" (II Peter 1:4).

Promise 1: *"Never will I leave you; never will I
forsake you" (Hebrews 13:5b).*

Christ promises that He will always be with you.
No matter where you are or what you are doing,
He is there. His Spirit lives inside of every believer
strengthening, encouraging, empowering, teaching,
and comforting. You will never be without the presence of God. *"Where can I go from your Spirit?
Where can I flee from your presence? If I go up to
the heavens, you are there; if I make my bed in the
depths, you are there. If I rise on the wings of the
dawn, if I settle on the far side of the sea, even there
your hand will guide me, your right hand will hold
me fast. If I say, "Surely the darkness will hide me
and the light become night around me," even the
darkness will not be dark to you; the night will shine
like the day, for darkness is as light to you" (Psalm
139:7-12).*

Promise 2: *"No temptation has seized you except
what is common to man. And God is faithful; he
will not let you be tempted beyond what you can
bear. But when you are tempted, he will also provide*

a way out so that you can stand up under it" (I Corinthians 10:13).

God promised that He will never allow any trial or temptation to overcome you, but will always provide a way for you to resist the temptations that come your way. *"When tempted, no one should say, 'God is tempting me.' For God cannot be tempted by evil, nor does he tempt anyone; but each one is tempted when, by his own evil desire, he is dragged away and enticed. Then, after desire has conceived, it gives birth to sin; and sin, when it is full-grown, gives birth to death" (James 1:13-15).* We are tempted when we are drawn away from God and His perfect will for our lives by Satan, the world, and even our old sinful nature. These enemies of ours can be very powerful forces, but God is infinitely more powerful.

When God allows temptation in your life, it is always for the strengthening and proving of your faith and His glory. Every single year before our May performance, we encounter "impossible" obstacles. At the time, I hate the hardships and am always tempted to despair and give up. But looking back, God has never let us down and has always used those difficulties to build the faith of the girls, their parents, the faculty, and me.

Promise 3: *"I can do everything through him who gives me strength" (Philippians 4:13).*

One of the best things about the Christian life is that you do not have to depend on your own strength and power. God promises in II Corinthians 12:10 that in your weakness His strength can be appropriated.

Because He lives inside of you, you have the strength that you need to do what He wants you to do. *"His divine power has given us everything we need for life and godliness through our knowledge of him who called us by his own glory and goodness" (II Peter 1:3).*

An airplane is just a big bucket of bolts that is bound by the laws of gravity and drag. It has wings and motors and everything else needed to fly, but will sit motionless on the runway unless the motor is started. As the plane moves forward, the shape of the wings causes the air current to travel over the top of the wings faster than the air that travels under them, creating greater air pressure underneath than on top. This lift is greater than gravity and causes the contraption to come off the ground. When gravity is overcome, the plane appears to be free. Does the law of gravity cease to exist? No. If the plane ceased to move, the air pressure would become equal on both sides of the wings, the power of lift would cease, and the plane would drop.

This is an illustration of what happens in your life. The law of gravity can be likened to the sinful nature. Before you become a Christian, you had no power to overcome the downward pull of your sinful nature. When Christ came and lived in you, He gave you the power to overcome the old, natural man. As with the principles of aerodynamics, there are certain rules that must be followed if the plane is to overcome the law of gravity. But if these "laws" are ignored, by folding the wings, for instance, the plane would no longer fly. If you ignore God's laws and choose not to appropriate His Spirit to live rightly, then you are subject to the power of the old nature. The sinful nature takes over and you fall.

The first thirteen verses of Romans 8 clearly contrast those who follow their sinful nature and those who walk after the Spirit. The former have their minds set on their own selfish, self-centered desires while the latter concentrate on what the Spirit desires, resulting in life and peace. Those controlled by their sinful nature do not belong to Christ and, therefore, cannot please God. When you become a Christian, the sinful nature is not eradicated, but its power over you is broken. The strength of the sinful nature is weakened as it is starved and subdued.

Frank uses an illustration of two hungry dogs representing our new and old natures. The stronger dog, and the one that wins the fight, is the one that is fed. You starve the sinful nature's control by the power of the Spirit within you Who enables you to make right choices. And it is the Bible that shows the right choices and how to make them.

CONDEMNED?
(written after Frank's sermon on Romans 8)

Condemned am I? Oh, no! 'Tain't so!
Christ solved that problem long ago.
He broke those iron gates of sin
That had my helpless soul locked in!
He stood between God's wrath and me
And took my place so willingly.
He bore that cross – He bore my shame
He died to justify my name.

Now, world, just say, what right have you,
To tell my heart what I should do?
To make me feel so incomplete
If I don't worship at your feet,
When Heaven's gate has opened wide
And swept this God-bought child inside;
Wherein I dwell, for now, by faith
While all its glories I embrace.

So how could I contented be
To walk in flesh like earthly men,
When I can, by the Spirit, soar
And live my life for sin no more?
When I can touch the Throne of God
'Though still upon this earth I trod;
When I can know my path shall lie
In sovereign goodness till I die.[1]

Frank has another good illustration related to overcoming the sinful nature. Suppose I hear your screaming and run into the room to see a vicious-looking man attacking you. He has you pinned to the floor, choking you. I go over and, with an expertly placed karate chop, break his back. You continue to yell for help because, even though the broken back renders the man powerless, the heaviness of his body remains on you. You still **feel** like he is killing you, even if it is not true. I tell you to throw him off because his power is broken. To experience the freedom you desire, you must push him away. The attacker is just like your sinful nature. Its power over you was broken when you became a Christian, but it is still present in you until you die and go to heaven. Until that time, you must minimize its impact in your life by throwing it off and choosing to follow God. Every time you obey the Lord, you weaken your sinful nature's stronghold over you; but when you disobey, sin's grip becomes stronger.

Promise 4: *"And my God will meet all your needs according to his glorious riches in Christ Jesus" (Philippians 4:19).*

Does it make sense that He Who spared not His Son for you, would leave any lesser need in your life unmet (Romans 8:32)? Whether the need is power to overcome temptation or the provision of ballet costumes, God will be Jehovah-Jirah, the Lord Who provides.

Every January we order costumes for the May ballet. One year in March, all of the costume companies called and said our orders could not be filled until June, which would be weeks after our scheduled spring performance. I began to wonder if maybe God just wanted us to have a Praise Concert that year rather than the elaborate story ballet that we usually did. But as I prayed, I felt God's leading me to trust Him for the costumes so the girls would witness His provision.

After calling every dressmaker in town and finding them all busy, I came to the conclusion that there was no human way for us to get the costumes we needed. I thought, "Lord, how in the world are You going to supply?" In a panic I prayed about changing the focus of the performance, but again felt the Lord was assuring me He would provide. Although I did not know how He would do it, I felt like He was leading us to quietly trust Him for the costumes without making our need public.

One morning I was about to start rehearsal when one of the mothers called me over and told me she had studied Acts 8 in her quiet time that morning. Not knowing why, she felt God wanted her to pray those particular verses for me. It was the story of Peter's raising Dorcas from the dead. I immediately thought that maybe this message of resurrection related to my painful back, since I was scheduled for surgery after the performance. But suddenly it hit me, "We have a situation with our costumes that is 'deader' than Dorcas, and we need a resurrection miracle."

Her eyes widened as she said, "Barbara, Dorcas was a seamstress." I didn't know **how** God was going to answer, but I had a renewed confidence that He **would**.

Someone came to me the next weekend and suggested that I ask Mark Horton to help. Mark Horton is a nationally known costume designer for ballet and theatre companies. I said, "Yeah, sure, I'll call him up out of the blue and say this is Barbara Barker in Birmingham, Alabama. Will you come and help us make 500 costumes?" How foolish would that sound? The next thought that came was, *"You do not have because you do not ask God" (James 4:2b).*

Believing God was directing, I called Mark's mother in Mississippi and asked her how to get in touch with him. Her quick response of "Oh, he's here" caught me completely off guard. My faith and courage were so small I never expected to get that far. When he immediately came to the phone, without having time to prepare a speech, I fumbled through my request. Instead of hearing, "Now, who are you?" I was shocked to hear, "I would love to." What I did not know at the time was that he was in Jackson making costumes for a city-wide ball. He had finished the project the night before and had told the Lord he wanted opportunities to serve Him with his skills. God's hand was all over these circumstances because Mark had been scheduled to do a wedding in Ireland during April and May and it had just been cancelled. That very week he came over to Birmingham, met with us, and caught the vision of our ballet.

The next week he returned with the most wonderful costume sketches. I then sent a letter to all of the dancers' parents telling them the story of our "miracle of Dorcas." I explained the need for all kinds of volunteers. Within a few days two big rooms at Briarwood were turned into "sweatshops" with sewing machines lined up along the walls. Volunteers poured in from everywhere. Mark measured every child and made the patterns for each individual costume. Others cut out the fabric and even more were at the machines sewing as fast as they could go.

I walked in one night and there at one of the machines sat the head of Anesthesiology at the University of Alabama at Birmingham, sewing a costume. He said, "I knew God was doing something here and I wanted to be a part." Although it was touch and go right up until the performance, God did it and the costumes were finished on time. Never was the ballet more beautifully costumed. God is seldom early, but never late.

God is seldom early, but never late.

And on and on I could go recounting God's provision for all of my weaknesses and needs. Sometimes He provides by using the Body of Christ to comfort, counsel, support, challenge, encourage, and help bear the burdens. Sometimes He provides for my needs apart from the help of others. And then sometimes He leaves my felt needs unmet to make me realize that my greatest need is simply to trust Him! But the final word is that I must look to God and Him alone to be my strength and help in all circumstances.

In conclusion, the God who called us to Himself, gives us every resource needed to resist the downward pull of the sinful nature and to live completely in obedience to Him. His power is always available and He orchestrates life events in such a way that we will never be in a position to fail. So why do hard things happen? The next chapter tells us.

MY PRAYER

Dear Lord, I know that you allow hard times in my life for Your purposes. Please help me to always remember that truth. When the temptations come, I pray for the strength to quickly resist. I also ask for the discipline to stay in the Word so that the godly nature will be strengthened and the sinful nature will weaken. Amen.

Notes

[1] Barker, Barbara B.

Chapter 10
PERSONAL APPLICATION

1. Have you ever felt totally defeated by your circumstances? Why?

2. Is there a particular area in your life in which you feel defeated or feel that the enemy has a foothold? After studying this lesson, what can you do?

Chapter 10
BIBLE STUDY

When we are tempted to feel that God is not there for us, what is the reality?

- Isaiah 43:2
- Psalm 16:8
- Psalm 73:23-26
- Psalm 145:18
- Matthew 28:20
- Acts 17:26-28

When we feel like we cannot resist a particular temptation, what does God say?

- I Corinthians 10:13
- II Chronicles 16:9
- Romans 6:13-14
- II Peter 3:17-18

What is the connection between being angry and giving the devil a foothold (Ephesians 4:26-27)?

The Greek word for foothold is *topos*, which can be interpreted as "opportunity" or "inhabitable space." Is there an area of your life in which you've allowed the enemy "squatter's rights"?

We are active participants in a spiritual battle, whether we realize it or not. Read Ephesians 6:10-18 and discuss each piece of armor and its function in equipping us for spiritual battle.

- Belt of truth

- Breastplate of righteousness

- Feet fitted with the gospel of peace

- Shield of faith

- Helmet of salvation

- Sword of the Spirit

- Prayer

How is God's power perfected in us (II Corinthians 12:9-10)?

God gives each believer His Holy Spirit and the power to resist temptation. Write out Philippians 4:13 in your own words.

According to Philippians 4:19, which of your needs will God meet? How will He meet them?

Read Matthew 6:25-34. Why should we not worry? What does God promise to His children?

Explain the meaning of Romans 8:32 and how it applies to your life.

According to I Peter 5:6, when will God lift you up?

Chapter 10
DISCUSSION QUESTIONS

1. In relation to resisting temptation, we have learned that there are things God does/will do and things He expects us to do. What are they?
   God:

   You:

2. Do you have a friend that is struggling with a sin area or a discouraging place in his/her life? How can you encourage him or her with the truths you have just learned?

3. Give some practical examples of how you can use spiritual armor.

CHAPTER 11

Suffering Is the Sculpting Tool of God

One of the least popular and often ignored promises of Christ is this: *"In this world you will
have trouble. But take heart! I have overcome the
world" (John 16:33b).* None of us desires the agony
of disappointment, pain, and all other manner of
distresses that plague us throughout our lives, but we
have to admit that God uses those times greatly to
strip us of ourselves, make us like Him, and use us in
the lives of others.

There is false teaching in certain segments of the
Church today that says suffering is not God's will
and is from the enemy; therefore, we should pray
against all forms of sickness and difficulties. Now,
for sure, Scripture instructs us to pray for deliver-
ance from evil and to be kept from the hand of the
enemy. And there are many examples in the Bible
when people prayed and God delivered and healed.
It is not wrong to ask for God to move mountains in

order to lead us to the green pastures where our souls may be refreshed and replenished. But we are fallen creatures living in a fallen world and are not exempt from the natural consequences of man's sinful nature and, for various reasons, God allows hard things to come into our lives. *"He . . . sends rain on the righteous and the unrighteous" (Matthew 5:45b).*

For the Christian, the news is great! Jesus Christ came and lived in our fallen world – and faced every trial and temptation that we shall ever experience: *"For we do not have a high priest who is unable to sympathize with our weaknesses, but we have one who has been tempted in every way, just as we are – yet was without sin" (Hebrews 4:15).* And then after walking through this fallen world without sin, He died on a cross and won an amazing victory over the god of this world, disarming him of every weapon designed to harm us. *"And having disarmed the powers and authorities, He made a public spectacle of them, triumphing over them by the Cross." (Colossians 2:15)* Because Christ won that victory, we who believe in Him have been delivered from the control and dominion of Satan. In addition, because of our relationship with God, we have access to the same authority by which He now rules over all principalities and powers. The power that raised Him from the dead now resides and works in us! (Ephesians 1:19-22).

Scripture clearly teaches that God allows difficulties for His glory and our good. Just look at the lives of Job, Abraham, Moses, Joseph, David, Jeremiah, and Paul, to name a few. Every person in

Scripture whom God chose for His instrument first went through the crucible of testing. Through difficult times He molded them and stripped them of their own self-sufficiencies, thus making them suitable for His service. If we too desire to be used by God, we must see hard times from His perspective and submit to His disciplining in the same manner. We begin to have the right perspective by knowing how we should **not** respond:

1. Do not be caught off-guard when trials come.

"Dear friends, do not be surprised at the painful trial you are suffering, as though something strange were happening to you" (I Peter 4:12). ". . . we must go through many hardships to enter the kingdom of God" (Acts 14:22b).

Many Christians are walking around with a false belief that if they live "good" lives, serving Him to the best of their ability, God will reward them and insolate them from hardships. First, we have to remember that there are no "good" people (Romans 3:12). The only goodness that we exhibit is that which comes from Christ. Secondly, the reason we should live rightly is to express our appreciation to God for His blessings, not to earn His goodness to us. And finally, we rest in the fact that God has a purpose for everything that He allows in our lives.

2. Do not judge God as being "unfair" and do not ask, "Why me?"

When we truly understand what we deserve from God and are only unworthy recipients of His grace and mercy, the real question we should ask is, "Why has God blessed me so much?" How many times have we been shown grace and mercy when what we really deserved was His judgment? *"He does not treat us as our sins deserve or repay us according to our iniquities. For as high as the heavens are above the earth, so great is his love for those who fear him" (Psalm 103:10-11). "What has happened to us is a result of our evil deeds and our great guilt, and yet, our God, you have punished us less than our sins have deserved and have given us a remnant like this" (Ezra 9:13).*

So the correct question is not, "Why do bad things happen to good people?", but "Why do good things happen to bad people?" If you really think about it, we are in no position to ever expect any good thing to come in our lives.

My sister, Anita, had a fifteen-year-old daughter, Barbara Lovelace, nicknamed Love. She was the all-American girl and adored by everyone. I loved my namesake dearly. She was in my high school girls' Bible class and her love for Jesus was obvious to all. One summer I noticed a progressive change in the unusual requests on her prayer cards. While most girls her age were asking me to pray for boyfriends and such, she wrote, "Help me to know Your voice." The next week it was, "Help me to accept Your will for me, no matter what it is," and the third week, "Help me to show love at home." Then one week I asked her what I should pray for her. With the most peaceful look, she said she did not have any more requests. All she wanted was to see Jesus and sit at

His feet, worshipping Him forever. And when we prayed together that day, her prayer seemed as though she was standing in the throne room of heaven.

The very next night she was in an automobile accident and went to be with the Lord. In reading her journals after her death, we saw how God had supernaturally told her she would die.

At the hospital as we waited for the doctor to give us his report, I looked at my sister and saw a countenance of serene peace. The doctor came out grief-stricken and said, "I'm sorry, there wasn't anything we could do."

I felt my world crumbling, but my sister went over to the doctor and putting her hand on his arm, said, "You mustn't be sad. This is not tragedy, but triumph. All we have ever wanted was for our children to trust Christ and live with Him forever." Angels filled the room that night.

Over the next few weeks we saw God work in many people's lives. The doctor in the emergency room and the policeman at the scene of the accident both came to know the Lord. On and on the stories went of how God used Love's death to draw people to Himself.

Anita, even in the midst of deep sorrow, triumphed in this tragedy by not blaming God for taking Love from her. Instead, she celebrated the goodness of the Lord, who gave her Love for a time, drew her to Himself, and then ushered her into His eternal presence.

3. Do not automatically see every trial as a punishment from God.

Although trials sometimes result from our own disobedience or bad choices, they are not always a form of judgment or discipline. Jesus Christ bore the eternal punishment that we deserve. So for the child of God, His correction takes the form of "chastisement," or "straightening," which will always result in our good in the end. Sometimes He uses people, circumstances, or even Satan himself, as His "rod of chastisement" to accomplish His purposes in our lives. But we are assured that we are always in the hand of God and nothing can touch us, for good or evil, without His permission. *"Do not be afraid of those who kill the body but cannot kill the soul. Rather, be afraid of the one who can destroy both soul and body in hell. Are not two sparrows sold for a penny? Yet not one of them will fall to the ground apart from the will of your Father. And even the very hairs of your head are all numbered. So don't be afraid; you are worth more than many sparrows"* (Matthew 10:28-31). *"Remember how the LORD your God led you all the way in the desert these forty years, to humble you and to test you in order to know what was in your heart, whether or not you would keep his commands. He gave you manna to eat in the desert, something your fathers had never known, to humble and to test you so that in the end it might go well with you"* (Deuteronomy 8:2, 16).

4. Do not think trials and tribulations only come in the form of severe happenings.

As a matter of fact, every day there are little trials (e.g., inconveniences, hurt feelings, interruptions, and failures to get your own way) to be faced with the same good attitude and patience that is required in the big ones. It is important that we learn to be faithful in small ways in order to assure our victory in the more difficult ones when they come. *"Whoever can be trusted with very little can also be trusted with much, and whoever is dishonest with very little will also be dishonest with much. . ." (Luke 16:10).* Hudson Taylor, founder of the China Inland Mission, once said, "A little thing is a little thing, but faithfulness in a little thing is a big thing."[1] It requires the same power of God to endure those little annoyances as it does the larger ones. God's power strengthens us for great endurance and patience in every circumstance (Colossians 1:11).

> *Hudson Taylor: "A little thing is a little thing, but faithfulness in a little thing is a big thing."* [1]

In addition to remembering what we are **not** to do, there are also truths we must equally consider as they relate to the trials in our life:

1. **Remember that God, Who called us before the foundation of the world to be made like Christ, uses the trials in our lives to bring about this conformation.**

There once was a sculptor who was carving a horse from a very large block of marble. Someone asked him how he went about transforming the marble into a horse. He replied, "Well, I look at the block and begin chiseling away everything that does not look like a horse." It is God's love for us that initiates the chastening designed to "sculpt" us into His image. *"For he chose us in him before the creation of the world to be holy and blameless in his sight"* (Ephesians 1:4). *"Blessed is the man you discipline, O LORD, the man you teach from your law"* (Psalm 94:12).

"So don't feel sorry for yourselves. Or have you forgotten how good parents treat children, and that God regards you as his children? My dear child, don't shrug off God's discipline, but don't be crushed by it either. It's the child he loves that he disciplines; the child he embraces, he also corrects. God is educating you; that's why you must never drop out. He's treating you as dear children. This trouble you're in isn't punishment; it's training, the normal experience of children. Only irresponsible parents leave children to fend for themselves. Would you prefer an irresponsible God? We respect our own parents for training and not spoiling us, so why not embrace God's training so we can truly live? While we were children, our parents did what seemed best to them. But God is doing what is best for us, training

us to live God's holy best. At the time, discipline isn't much fun. It always feels like it's going against the grain. Later, of course, it pays off handsomely, for it's the well-trained who find themselves mature in their relationship with God" (Hebrews 12:5-11 The Message).

2. **Remember that trials and afflictions cause us to lose confidence in anything or anybody but Him.**

As a result, He is free to work in our lives for our good and His glory. *"In this you greatly rejoice, though now for a little while (a season – KJV) you may have had to suffer grief in all kinds of trials. These have come so that your faith—of greater worth than gold, which perishes even though refined by fire—may be proved genuine and may result in praise, glory and honor when Jesus Christ is revealed" (I Peter 1:6-7). "Consider it pure joy, my brothers, whenever you face trials of many kinds, because you know that the testing of your faith develops perseverance. Perseverance must finish its work so that you may be mature and complete, not lacking anything" (James 1:2-4).*

In Deuteronomy 8 God explains that He allows hard times in our lives so that we will not become prideful and self-reliant. When everything is going smoothly and all of our needs and wants are satisfied, we have a tendency to forget that God is the source of all the goodness. Difficulties are there to make us depend on Him and not on ourselves. Not only will they show us what really matters, but they have a way of revealing what is in our hearts.

3. **Remember that all the trials that He allows in our lives are tempered by His hand as to duration and severity.**

He stands as the refiner by the fire, carefully watching as the impurities are burned out of the gold ore. *"He will sit as a refiner and purifier of silver; he will purify the Levites and refine them like gold and silver" (Malachi 3:3a).* When He sees His reflection, He knows the temperature is just right. He understands what is necessary to perfect His treasure, and His gaze is never diverted. As we learned in the last chapter: *"No temptation has seized you except what is common to man. And God is faithful; He will not let you be tempted beyond what you can bear. But when you are tempted, He will also provide a way out so that you can stand up under it" (I Corinthians 10:13). "But He knows the way that I take; when He has tested me, I will come forth as gold" (Job 23:10).*

Sometimes it appears that God is allowing Satan to have free reign in ours lives. You must remember that he is a defeated foe and under the complete, sovereign control of our loving Father. I often say, "Satan can only build a stage on which God does a greater work."

Satan can only build a stage
on which God does a greater work.

4. **He promises to go with us through the trials and afflictions, strengthen our hearts, and draw us closer to Himself as we endure them.**

"But now, this is what the LORD says- he who created you, O Jacob, he who formed you, O Israel: 'Fear not, for I have redeemed you; I have summoned you by name; you are mine. When you pass through the waters, I will be with you; and when you pass through the rivers, they will not sweep over you. When you walk through the fire, you will not be burned; the flames will not set you ablaze'" (Isaiah 43:1-2). "So do not fear, for I am with you; do not be dismayed, for I am your God. I will strengthen you and help you; I will uphold you with my righteous right hand" (Isaiah 41:10).

For several summers I taught ballet in the inner city at the Center for Urban Missions, using it as a conduit for teaching the children the truths of God. What I wanted most was to give them opportunities to see God work. One particular year, I had about 20 children from five to ten years old who were, to say the least, behaviorally challenged. We met in a very large, non-air-conditioned room of the community center in an inner-city housing project. Loud fans circulated hot air and doors opened into the halls where other activities were taking place. It was a noisy, chaotic atmosphere.

On the first day, I finally got the kids calmed down, went to turn on the praise music which I would use for the class, and found the cassette player would not work. I tried everything, but soon realized I needed to turn my attention to the kids before they were totally out of control. So for the entire class we danced as I sang the praise music. By the end of the day, I was exhausted from singing and doing my best to tame those energetic little children.

Before I went back the next day, I made sure the tape player worked, but when I turned it on at the community center the tape broke. The third day I decided to take a record player, which I carefully checked out before I left. I got the kids settled and tried to click it on. It would not work! The director of the program came over to help, but he could not fix it. A maintenance man looked at it and said the switch was jammed underneath and the player would have to be dismantled.

Then it hit me, "This isn't an accident. Once was a problem, twice was a coincidence, but three times had to be of Satan. The music is what calms the spirits of the children and opens the door for me to point them to God. It is obvious the enemy does not want this to happen." I remembered the verse: *"He who does what is sinful is of the devil, because the devil has been sinning from the beginning. The reason the Son of God appeared was to destroy the devil's work" (I John 3:8).*

It was like God spoke to my heart and said, "Ask Me to fix the record player." My heart sank. Did He really want me to step out and trust Him to fix the player?

"Do you believe I came to destroy the works of the devil?" He asked in that still, small voice.

What could I say but, "Yes, I do, Lord," although I was not personally convinced. But at that moment I had such a conviction that if I didn't turn around and tell the children what He was showing me, I would be in disobedience.

So I turned to the children and said, "Kids, the music that we wanted to play for the past three days praised God. But the devil can't stand it. There is a verse in the Bible that tells us that Jesus came to destroy the works of the devil. I think that the devil does not want us to dance and praise Jesus and he is keeping our record player from working."

I was saying the words, but not at all believing He was going to fix the player. I continued, "So we're going to pray and ask God to overcome the devil's work and fix this record player." I said a prayer and then turned around to start the music, all the time preparing a little speech about how God sometimes answers prayer "yes" and sometimes He answers "no." But when I clicked the switch, the record began playing. I was stunned. The children's eyes were as big as saucers and, for the first time all week, there was total silence. They were in the palm of my hand for the rest of the summer.

We put on a program at the end for the parents. All anyone could talk about was the miracle God did with the record player. I will not know until I get to heaven all the ways God used that one little miracle to build the faith of those children and their parents. But we would have never seen God work if we had not first experienced the trial.

As insignificant as a broken record player may seem, it is in the little things that we learn to apply God's truths, thus preparing us for the larger challenges that will come our way. Jesus said in Luke 16:10: *"Whoever can be trusted with very little can also be trusted with much . . ."*

5. **Remember God's faithfulness of the past while going through the trials.**

Over and over in the Old Testament God reminded the Israelites of all the ways He protected and provided for them in the past as a way to encourage them in their present difficulty. This same principle can work for us today. How has God met your needs during past difficulties? When you lost your job, did you ever go hungry? When your husband died, did you experience the peace that cannot be explained? Did He not restore your joy? As we remember how God worked in past trials, we will gain confidence that He will not fail us in our present circumstances.

One day Frank found me literally crying over the checkbook as I realized that I had more month left at the end of my money. He said, "Honey, what's wrong?"

With my typical martyr spirit I replied, "There's no way to make the money stretch when you give it all away. I don't see how we can pay all of these bills." And on and on I went, lamenting over our lack of funds.

Later that day, he came home and I was happily singing. Puzzled by my abrupt change of attitude, he asked me, "Did we get an inheritance?"

In between the time that he had left and returned, I "happened" to receive in the mail a cassette tape of my recent talk to a group in Chattanooga. During the talk I had recounted several of my "faith" stories, of how God had repeatedly met our needs when I had seen no possible provision. That day as I sat and listened to myself and recalled the incidents of which I spoke, I remembered how He had never failed to provide **in** time and **on** time. My spirit lifted as I diverted my focus from my present situation to my faithful and all-sufficient God. And somehow, in ways I cannot particularly remember now, the bills were paid by the end of the month, just like they always were.

6. **Remember that standing faithfully and victoriously in trials and afflictions is a learning process.**

Along the way we may stumble and fall and may even fail, but even if we are unfaithful, He will remain faithful. As with all sin, forgiveness and restoration are only a confession away. We must hold fast to the truths which He has given and continually bring our thoughts into captivity to the Word of God (II Corinthians 10:4-5) and not give up – because He never gives up on us.

7. **Remember that God prepares us to be used as His instruments to comfort others who are suffering, pointing them to the goodness and sufficiency of God.**

In II Corinthians 1:3-4 Paul says, *". . . the God of all comfort, who comforts us in all our troubles, so that we can comfort those in any trouble with comfort we ourselves have received from God."* When we receive comfort from God, we are equipped to pass this same comfort on to others. Another's particular trial does not have to be the same as ours; the basic principles still apply. Troubles may vary, but the comfort is the same because the comfort is based on the attributes of God Who never changes. Suffering is a training ground for service to the Body of Christ. Our lives are so intertwined that what impacts one, impacts all.

Several years ago I began having seizures that were so bad on some nights Frank had to hold my legs down until the seizures subsided. After all kinds of tests, the doctors still could not explain the source of my problem. Soon the seizures started coming more frequently, with increasing intensity. A really bad one struck while I was driving in rush-hour traffic. Young Frank, who was about twelve at the time, got out of the car and stuck his thumb out. It "just so happened" that a member of Briarwood drove by, saw Frank III, and stopped. They rushed me to the hospital where the doctors again ran all kinds of tests, but they still could not agree on what was wrong.

In the weeks before my seizures started, the enemy seemed to be attacking our church in a really concentrated way. Several issues had arisen that threatened to divide the congregation, but God intervened and brought unity. I watched as He provided unbelievable, supernatural protection each time. Then it looked like the enemy was after Frank personally.

One night Frank came in looking a little rattled, sat down and said, "I think Satan is trying to kill me." Now Frank is not one to talk like that. He began telling me of some things that had occurred recently and then related what had happened that night. While driving on a four lane road, a truck in the opposite lane aimed directly for him. He ran his car off the road and into the ditch. Immediately he looked around and saw no truck. Well, that scared the daylights out of me.

After several months, it suddenly dawned on me that maybe God was using my seizures to get at Frank. He was becoming terribly distracted from his ministry. Several times a day he called just to check up on me, which was not at all like him.

Then one night, as I experienced the oncoming of another seizure, I felt led to call on the name of Jesus Christ and refuse the enemy access to my body. It seemed like I was in an intense spiritual battle where I fought the enemy in hand-to-hand combat. Miraculously, the seizure subsided. From then on, every time one threatened, I entered in the same kind of intense struggle, keeping my eyes focused on Jesus, the Author and Perfecter of my faith (Hebrews 12:1-3).

Not too long after, I was scheduled to go on a speaking trip, which was to last for several days and cover several cities. I had cancelled previous trips out of fear of having a seizure away from home, but I felt that if I believed God's victory was available to me, I had to make this trip. As I left from the Atlanta airport, I felt the beginnings of a seizure. Holding onto the Lord with all I had, I fought it and fought it. I demanded, in the name of the Lord Jesus, that Satan not touch me. That seizure subsided; however, three times during the trip the seizures returned and the spiritual struggle was so intense I nearly gave up and went home. But each time the thought came, "If you go home, you've given in," which I was determined not to do.

Finally, I reached Charlotte, North Carolina, my last stop. By that time I was very weak, spiritually as well as physically. I stood to speak for this last time and had the strange sensation that something drained from my body. I knew the seizures were gone. And they never came back. I do not want to make it sound like every illness is from the devil. But I had gone to many doctors and not one had come up with a good explanation of what was happening to me. The only other possible reason was the enemy was behind them.

A member of our church experienced brain damage in a terrible car wreck. As a result, she had severe seizures which were coming more and more frequently, up to five or six a day. She did not want to go anywhere for fear of having one while she was in public. But for some reason, she felt led to come to a particular retreat where I was speaking. She slipped in the back and I was not even aware she was there. I had not planned on it, but I found myself recounting, for the first time, the story of my seizures. As she listened, a seizure began. She called on the name of Jesus and rebuked the enemy. Right at that moment she was assured in her spirit that the seizures were gone for good.

Many times Satan uses physical ailments to get us out of the spiritual battle. It is understandable; when we feel bad, our focus is on our discomfort and not God. We have a tendency to give into the pain and tiredness without waiting on God to lift us above them. Have you allowed physical pain to keep you from serving God? If so, ask God to show His intentions in allowing your illness or your struggle. He will either give the victory to endure it with patience and joyfulness or show you to rebuke Satan for any part he has in it. Sometimes God takes it away and sometimes He does not. Remember that God's plan is not to heal all the time.

Do not look to others' situations with the expectation that God will work the same way in your life. What He has planned for one may be completely different than what He has planned for another. One thing for sure, Satan cannot touch God's own without God's permission, and God's permission is given only when it accomplishes what is good for us and ultimately brings glory to Himself.

Not all illnesses are from the enemy. God's plan may be to allow pain as His instrument to help you grow. James said, beginning in chapter one, verse two, *"Consider it pure joy, my brothers, whenever you face trials of many kinds, because you know that the testing of your faith develops perseverance. Perseverance must finish its work so that you may be mature and complete, not lacking anything."*

I have lived with horrible back pain for years, enduring several surgeries and even more nerve blocks. Although I prayed for healing, God, in His sovereignty, chose not to heal me completely. I have learned to use the pain as a way of thanking the Lord for His strength. Also, I have learned to be thankful my eyes work, my heart beat is regular, and I have no problem with my hearing. I do not have headaches or arthritis and my blood pressure is normal. There are far more things right with me than broken. My focus is on what works, not on what does not. Why should I complain about one thing when I have all of these other things to be thankful for?

Why should I focus on one little thorn? Remember what Scripture says about God's purpose in regards to thorns. According to II Corinthians 12, they are there so we won't exalt ourselves (verse 7). Why does God not take them away? They make us appropriate His strength (verse 9). As a result Paul said he delighted in difficulties because he knew that when he was weak, God made him strong (verse 10). Have you come to the place in your life where you can trust Him with the thorns God allows?

In difficult circumstances, I always fall back on what I refer to as "the trinity of truths":

- **God loves me.** The evidence of this is that He sent Jesus. *"He who did not spare his own Son, but gave him up for us all—how will he not also, along with him, graciously give us all things?" (Romans 8:32).*

- **God is sovereign.** Matthew 10:29-31 says, *"Are not two sparrows sold for a penny? Yet not one of them will fall to the ground apart from the will of your Father. And even the very hairs of your head are all numbered. So don't be afraid; you are worth more than many sparrows."*

- **God is in control.** *"And we know that in all things God works for the good of those who love him, who have been called according to his purpose" (Romans 8:28).*

As a result I experience the peace that cannot be understood from a human perspective: *"And the peace of God, which transcends all understanding, will guard your hearts and your minds in Christ Jesus" (Philippians 4:7).*

CRUCIFIXION IS THE GOAL

Oh, heart, my foolish, sinful heart,
Brace yourself and listen to the Lord.
So what if all your dreams are crushed?
So what if what He asks of you is hard?
Don't you **know** that **crucifixion** is the goal?
Don't you know that self can never
share the throne?
Don't you **know** this life was never meant to be
A time to succor sins of flesh or make
this earth its home?
You've prayed for God to show the barriers
in your soul
That caused the vision of His face to be made dim,
So break, so bend, so give God's hand full sway –
And one day soon you'll be conformed to Him!!![3]

TEARS OF HOPE – BREAKING AND REMAKING

The tears won't stop; they come unbidden,
My broken heart cannot be hidden.
My friends are kind, their love is real,
But no one knows just how I feel.

The pain is hard; the pain is deep.
The pain won't quit; I cannot sleep.
I want to run; I want to hide.
I can't escape from what's inside.

I know it's God Who's breaking me.
And it's His hand that's shaking me.
But I have heard the things He breaks
He purposes to then remake.
And what He shakes revealing tares,
In holiness He will repair.

Then what is left is strong and pure,
And for His purpose will endure.
A vessel fit of purest gold,
One He can use with Christ its mold.

So finish then Your work in me
Until Your image You can see.
Just keep me, Lord, from failing You,
I feel so weak in all I do.

My head is full of all I've learned –
Please let me now Your will discern.
For matching head to hand and heart
Requires that You, Lord, strength impart.

For I am weak so bound in flesh,
So void of true holiness.
But 'tis my goal that it should be
Much more of Christ and less of me.

They come unbidden, my broken heart
Cannot be hidden.
My friends are kind, their love is real,
But no one knows just how I feel.

The pain is hard; the pain is deep.
The pain won't quit; I cannot sleep.
I want to run; I want to hide.
I can't escape from what's inside.
I know it's God Who's breaking me.

And it's His hand that's shaking me.
But I have heard the things He breaks
He purposes to then remake.
And what He shakes revealing tares,
In holiness He will repair.

Then what is left is strong and pure,
And for His purpose will endure.
A vessel fit of purest gold,
One He can use with Christ its mold.

So finish then Your work in me
Until Your image You can see.
Just keep me, Lord, from failing You,
I feel so weak in all I do.

My head is full of all I've learned –
Please let me now Your will discern.
For matching head to hand and heart
Requires that You, Lord, strength impart.

For I am weak so bound in flesh,
So void of true holiness.
But 'tis my goal that it should be
Much more of Christ and less of me.[4]

MY PRAYER

Dear Lord, please help me see trials from Your prospective. I know you are in total control of all that concerns me and you allow the hard times for my good and Your glory, but sometimes it is just plain hard to believe that when I am in pain. Also, give me opportunities to help others who are going through trials, both in word and deed. Amen.

Notes

[1] http://www.navigators.org/us/ministries/b2g/articles The%20 Call/items/Patches%20of%20Godlight (accessed 12-22-06).

[2] Barker, Barbara B.

[3] Ibid.

[4] Ibid.

Chapter 11
PERSONAL APPLICATION

1. Think back to the various trials you have gone through. How has God brought about good in your life and the lives of others as a result?

2. How could you have responded better?

3. How well are you prepared for future trials?

Chapter 11
BIBLE STUDY

Should we be surprised when trials come (I Peter 4:12)?

Should Paul have been surprised by his trials (Acts 9:15-16)?

What are some reasons/results for trials and sufferings according to the following verses?
- Job 5:17
- Psalm 119:67
- John 15:2
- Hebrews 12:11
- Psalm 66:10, Isaiah 48:10-11, Malachi 3:3
- I Peter 1:6-7
- James 1:2-4
- Romans 5:3-5
- II Corinthians 1:3-7
- II Corinthians 1:9
- Acts 16:25b

How should we respond (both attitudes and actions) in times of trial?
- Proverbs 3:11-12
- Jeremiah 10:23-24
- Hebrews 10:34
- I Thessalonians 5:17

- I Thessalonians 5:18
- James 1:2a

When the trial seems too great, what can you be assured of according to I Corinthians 10:13?

How does knowing that love is the motivating factor when God allows trials in our lives affect our response to them (Proverbs 3:12, Revelation 3:19)?

How does knowing that God is in control of **everything** affect your response to trials (Matthew 10:29-31)?

How does knowing that Christ is interceding for us affect our responses to trials (Hebrews 7:25, Luke 22:32)?

How should we pray for those going through trials (Colossians 1:11)?
(This is just one of many verses that you should pray.)

Chapter 11
DISCUSSION QUESTIONS

1. For those of you going through very difficult times: God must love you very much and also put much confidence in your faith to allow your suffering. Comment on this statement.

2. In what specific ways can you encourage a friend who is going through trials?

3. What things would **not** be good to say?

4. What can you do now to prepare for trials in the future?

CHAPTER 12

Bringing It All Together

Many people ask me how to walk by faith. Exercising faith is not difficult. Each one of us exercises faith every day. We trust in doctors' diagnoses, bridges to get us across rivers, weather and newspaper reports, and even those silly internet stories. The problem is the object of our faith (what we put our faith in).

Most Christians today live like practical atheists, constrained by their own weaknesses and limited in their vision of God. There are various reasons for this, such as a comfortable culture and weak Christian leadership, but it all boils down to not believing in who God is and that He is able to perform all He has promised. Martin Luther, the great reformer, said, "What greater rebellion, impiety, or insult to God can there be than not to believe His promises."[1] Romans 4:20-21 says of Abraham: *"Yet he (Abraham) did not waver through unbelief regarding the promise of God, but was strengthened in his faith and gave glory to God, being fully persuaded that God had power to do what he had promised."* Abraham and all those great men and women of the faith who have gone before relied on the promises of God. Walking by faith is simply demonstrating, through our actions, that we believe God's Word is true.

> ### *Martin Luther: "What great rebellion, impiety, or insult to God can there be than not to believe His promises."[1]*

I am the last person to get all self-righteous about walking by faith. Frank dragged me into this "trusting God" lifestyle rather reluctantly, to say the least. But now looking back on our wild, forty (plus) year journey on the emotional roller coaster of faith, I would not trade it for anything.

From the beginning of our marriage, Frank forced me to trust God for the impossible. At first I referred to it as his "presumptuous faith" and fought him every step of the way, sometimes threatening to leave him if he increased our financial pledge to the church one more time. But Frank's face was set like flint and he would not waiver from what he thought God had called him to do. As a result, we have seen God prove time after time that He will never fail.

Frank was so laid back in the way he trusted God for everything. "Honey, you either trust God or you don't," he would say. For many years I thought his simple faith was trivializing serious life-altering situations. But my opinion changed permanently right before our third child, Peggy, was born. That was when I finally started to believe the Lord would not abandon us.

Before that time, I was in a period of rebellion, especially about Frank's "generous stewardship." Right before Peggy came, I told him if he upped the pledge to the church again I was going to leave; even though, I knew I did not have anywhere to go. It was my opinion we could not afford to give away any more money. Our car was falling apart and we had a third baby on the way without the financial means to check out of the hospital. Ignoring my threat, he increased the pledge anyway. And I was furious.

Around that time, he led a Dodge dealer to the Lord and they began getting together for discipleship. One day it rained as Frank drove his very leaky car to their meeting. He was soaked by the time he got to the car dealership. After they finished their session, the man said, "Frank, I want to give you something, if you let me give it on my terms." Frank said sure. The dealer continued, "I want to give you a new car. It won't be yours; it will be our demonstrator. All you have to do is put gas and oil in it. We'll pay for everything else and replace it next year."

That very day Frank came home driving a beautiful white station wagon with baby blue interior and power windows. He said, "Honey, look what God gave us." I got so excited I went into labor.

The night before I was to go home from the hospital, I looked over at Frank relaxing in the chair and said, "Frank, we don't have the money we need to check out tomorrow."

In his irritatingly calm manner he said, "Honey, what are you worried about? We don't get out until tomorrow?" That really burned me up.

Although I saw God work time after time meeting our needs, I still feared that one day we would run out of money and I would have to go to my father and ask him to bail us out. Daddy did not approve of how we were living by faith, but he could not say anything because he saw how God provided. Anyway, later that evening, the Dodge dealer came by to see Frank with a check. We did not know it at the time, but the man had taken our old broken down car, fixed it up, and sold it. The sale price was $400 and our hospital bill "just happened to be" $396. God provided exactly what we needed with a little bit to spare.

I began with tentative baby steps of faith, but the true turning point came when I fed Sloppy Joes to a boys' fraternity. I was always a self-sufficient person and relatively successful in almost everything I attempted – and then I married Frank. Becoming a mother of three babies in two-and-a-half years was overwhelming to me. I had no experience with little children. On top of that, Frank wanted me to do things I could not do. He wanted to invite others over for dinner and I had never cooked. Even worse, he wanted to invite a lot of people! Teaching Sunday School was not a possibility because my "doctrines were not clearly defined," at that time. I could have danced, but no one wanted me to do that. I was not much of a reader, and other women would come over and talk with Frank about these great books they had read. I was envious of the lively discussions they had because I could not add a thing to their conversations. I tried to talk to people about Jesus and no one came to the Lord. Every area of my life seemed to be a failure. God had stripped me to the core.

After the day of brokenness and reconciliation with God (which I talked about in my testimony in the preface), I wanted to be an asset to my husband rather than a weight around his neck. But I had no idea how to do that. Frank was well-meaning, but not very helpful. He bluntly asked, "Well, honey, what can you do?"

Finally, I decided I could begin to contribute by letting Frank invite guests for dinner. He firmly believed ministry began in the home. Up until that time, I had resisted having people over because I could not cook and, in my eyes, our house was not fine enough for entertaining. When I was growing up, my mother had entertained very graciously in our beautiful home, with a cook in the kitchen and a gardener in the yard. This was very different from what I was capable of doing.

Allowing him to invite people for dinner was a difficult step for me because it required swallowing my pride and exposing my inadequacies. But I finally told Frank to go ahead and invite someone. He got so excited and told me of his plans to ask the teenage boys from his old high school fraternity. While in high school he had been the treasurer of this same fraternity and had stolen $25 of their money to pay off a gambling debt. Recently he had written a letter to them, confessed his thievery, given his testimony, and paid back the debt. This naturally opened a door to share the Gospel with those young men and a relationship began. His ultimate purpose for inviting them over for dinner was to tell them more about Jesus.

"You've got to be kidding," I told him. "I was thinking about two or three, not a whole fraternity. There is absolutely no way I can have a Mountain Brook fraternity in my house. I can't even cook!"

"But, honey, you *can do **all** things through Christ who strengthens you* (Philippians 4:13)," he replied.

"But we have no money," I argued, knowing that would not fly either.

As I expected, he came back with, *"And my God will meet all your needs according to his glorious riches in Christ Jesus" (Philippians 4:19).*

I hated it when he argued with me using Scripture. How could I ever win?

Anyway, I could not see how I was going to feed 30 boys, but I did not want to go back to the spiritual desert again. As I prayed about it, God showed me very clearly that obedience on my part would result in His blessing and provision. He also reminded me that He had not called me to **feel** like doing something; He had called me to **do** something. So I stepped out into that vulnerable place where I was willing to do His will.

Arrangements were made and the boys were scheduled to come for dinner the next Monday night. During the week some ladies at the church gave me the recipe for Sloppy Joes, but I still did not have money for the food. On Saturday an unexpected insurance refund check for $25 arrived in the mail, which I used to buy the ingredients needed to feed 33 people.

By 5:00 p.m. on Monday, the food was made with the money provided, the house was clean, and our three small children, ages 2 ½, 1 ½, and six-months, were unusually good. I was amazed at God's provision! Suddenly the boys started arriving. But something was not right. There were girls with them and to my horror there were a whole lot more than thirty.

One of the boys told Frank, "We thought we'd turn this into a rush party and bring dates."

"No problem," Frank replied. "Come on in." I could have killed him.

And with that, they started coming, and coming, and coming. Kids pressed through my tiny house until all of the rooms were filled. Some overflowed out the back door into the yard and others were sitting on the basement steps. They even filled our bathroom! That really ticked me off because I had planned to lock myself in there after the food ran out, leaving Frank to deal with the disaster.

Frank asked the blessing and I started serving. As the kids went through the line, I was so humiliated I would not even look at their faces. I just kept spooning Sloppy Joe sauce onto the buns on their plates. We ran out of buns and started using loaves of bread. We ran out of bread and somebody went next door to borrow some more. My hands were busy serving, but my mind was in overdrive as I composed angry speeches for Frank — and God. They had led me into this and I felt betrayed by both of them.

It had not dawned on me that we never ran out of Sloppy Joe sauce until I heard Frank say, "Does anybody want to come back for more?" I stepped back from the stove and realized that God had indeed met my needs. And miraculously at that! But more than multiplying the food, He had honored my willingness to step into the place where I lacked ability and resources and had provided everything I needed to feed 99 teenagers!

After that night, masses of teenagers came every week. Frank said if we fed them they would come and he was right. Eventually different people volunteered to have them in their homes, which resulted in the Bible Talk Supper Clubs. Over the years, hundreds of young people came to the Lord. Out of this ministry came small group Bible studies comprised of students from the area high schools.

I was the leader of one of the original small group Bible studies and wanted so much for the girls in my group to catch a vision of stepping out in faith and seeing God work the impossible through them. We were reading George Mueller's autobiography as a group and discussing how Mueller trusted God to provide for the orphanages he ran. I told them I was looking for a way that they could learn to trust God to use them to reach their peers for Christ. They suggested a coffeehouse.

My first reaction was negative. It was not like I needed something else to do. I had little children and, besides that, I did not know anything about running a coffeehouse. But after we prayed about it, I inadvertently found myself looking for a suitable place to rent for such a ministry.

One day I was in Mountain Brook Village, a shopping area in a suburb of Birmingham, and saw an abandoned, dilapidated building and thought that it would work. And besides, it looked like it would be cheap. The front porch was caved in and the wiring and plumbing did not work, but the layout was just right. I felt strongly that God was leading me to claim the place for Him.

When I went to the owner and asked how much the rent was, he asked me what I wanted to pay. I said I did not know because I was just going to ask the Lord to provide what we needed. Patronizingly, he sent me off and told me to come back when I had a figure.

I was puzzled as to what the amount should be and I did not know how to go about getting it. One of the commitments the kids and I had made in the beginning was to be like George Mueller and not let our needs be known to anyone except God. So I went home and prayed for a figure. The amount of $50 ran around in my head, but I did not know if it was from God or just a random thought. I asked God to make it clear if it was from Him. When I got to the teenagers' Bible study, one of the young girls asked me if the rent was $50 per month. How weird! I had not told anyone about that amount. Her mother had told her that if the rent was $50, she would give us the first three months. There was the figure and the provision.

Confident that God was orchestrating all of these events, I went and proposed the $50 amount to the owner. He responded, "Miss Barbara, we can't even pay the property taxes for less than $225 a month." That crushed me because I felt like I had missed God. I was confused because I had been so sure that God led me to that figure.

The next Saturday morning during the men's prayer breakfast at our home, a man asked me why I seemed down. I told him I felt like I had led the kids to step out and trust God and I had blown it. I recounted the story and went on to tell him how frustrated I was in not knowing how to proceed. He asked me how I planned to get the money after the first three months. I told him we would just trust God to provide. He looked at me and said, "Well, since you were going to trust God for $50 a month, couldn't you just as well trust Him to provide $225 a month?" His question stunned me. He continued, "Let me challenge you with this thought. Was it not true that you were willing to trust Him with $50 a month because if God hadn't come through, you felt like you could find a way to get that amount? But if the amount were greater than $50, you knew you couldn't cover it if God didn't come through. Do you really want to see God work?"

Later, as Frank and I prayed about it, we both felt God was leading us to go forward with the lease at $225 per month. But it was not just the rent for which we had to trust God; we also needed repairs and furnishings. As we prayed for God's provision for every little thing, the word got around. Calls came from everywhere offering help — one offered electrical services; one was a carpenter. Sears called and offered us damaged office furniture. Pasquales' Pizza closed and offered their tables and chairs. Sherwin Williams donated leftover paint and carpet came from a Central Bank renovation. So many people entered in and helped get the coffeehouse ready to open.

After a very exciting time of seeing God work, we were ready for opening night. We planned to offer hot chocolate, coffee, Russian tea, and soft drinks along with chips and sandwiches. There was a little stage for entertainment and an area to sell Christian books. A member of Briarwood who was Miss Alabama was to be the featured speaker.

But on Friday afternoon, before the opening on Saturday night, a city official came by and asked if we had permission from the zoning board to operate. I told him the owner said it was zoned church/school so we should be okay. He went on to say that a foot of the grassy area inside the property line was zoned residential, which meant we would need permission from the board before we opened. Unfortunately, the board would not meet until Monday night. My heart sank because all of the publicity was already out. But confident that God was in control, we prayed.

Frank's father, who was retired from the zoning board, said he would work on it. I asked the kids to pray Proverbs 21:1 *("The king's heart is in the hand of the LORD; he directs it like a watercourse wherever he pleases.")*, for God to guide the decision of the officials. On Friday evening I got a call from that same official who said they had discussed our situation and decided to go ahead and let us open, contingent on the board's decision on Monday. On opening night, the coffeehouse was a great success.

Monday night the zoning board deliberated and decided to let us continue on a probationary basis with the condition that none of the neighbors would complain. Their contingent decision turned out to be a blessing in disguise because it kept us on our best behavior.

When we opened, we charged admission of a quarter. Someone sat at the door with a basket. It did not look very official, so we missed collecting from most of the people. One night I was praying about the situation with hand motions, "Lord, we need a counter by the door, this high and this long, so we look official."

The next day I went to the church and a man came up to me and said, "We're moving into our new house and there is a bar in the basement this high and this long that we don't need. Do you want it?" His hands did just what I remember my hands doing when I had prayed. The bar he gave us, which we used as a counter, was perfect.

The coffeehouse ministry, initiated by the desire to move God's hands through prayer and faith, produced many opportunities for learning great principles from God. The teenagers saw God work in unique and supernatural ways to meet our needs and change the hearts of those that came through the doors. But after a time, God decided to take us down another path of faith.

The coffeehouse had been open for about eighteen months when the owner of the building decided to tear it down to make a parking lot. I was upset to see to the coffeehouse close because God was using it greatly in so many people's lives. But God was in control and I knew He would give us new opportunities to see Him work, which He did.

MY PRAYER

Dear Lord, more than anything I want to be Your instrument. Help me to trust You in every circumstance, to fix my eyes on You. I know with You all things are possible. Amen.

Notes

[1] Luther, Martin; *Concerning Christian Liberty*; translated by R. S. Grignon; http://www.iclnet.org/pub/resources/text/wittenberg/luther/web/cclib-2.html (accessed 12-22-06).

Chapter 12
PERSONAL APPLICATION

1. Has there been a time God prompted you to step out in faith and do something? Did you do it? What were the results?

2. Looking back, what were the reasons for your not stepping out in faith?

3. What about your life is extraordinary because you believe God?

Chapter 12
BIBLE STUDY

Using the following verses, describe faith in self and its results. What does God say about it?

- Jeremiah 9:23

- Daniel 4:30-32

- Proverbs 16:25

- Romans 1:21

- James 4:13-14

- Luke 12:19-20

- Galatians 6:3

- Revelation 3:17

When the disciples asked Jesus to increase their faith, what did He say (Matthew 17:20-21)?

What do we learn from His response?

How does the Bible define faith (Hebrews 11:1)?

Where does faith come from (Romans 10:17)?

What is the evidence of faith (James 2:17)?

Describe the enemies of faith and how you can defend against them.

- Enemy #1 (Matthew 4:1, Ephesians 6:12, John 8:44):
  - o Ephesians 6:11; 13-18

  - o James 4:7

  - o Matthew 4:4

  - o Ephesians 4:26-27

- Enemy #2 (John 15:19):
  - o John 16:33

  - o I Corinthians 3:19

  - o I John 2:15

  - o Mark 16:15

- Enemy #3 (Romans 7:18, Galatians 5:17)
  - o Romans 8:5

  - o Romans 13:14

o   Galatians 5:16

o   I Peter 4:2

Describe the three aspects of faith.
*   Saving faith – Ephesians 2:8-9

*   Persevering faith – II Corinthians 1:24b, Galatians 2:20, James 1:3

*   Aggressive faith – Philippians 4:13; I John 4:4 and 5:4; Matthew 17:20-21; Hebrews 11 (note verses 8-10)

What do you learn about faith from the following people?
*   Abraham (Genesis 22; Romans 4:18-21)

*   Joshua & Caleb (Numbers 13)

*   David (I Samuel 17)

*   Jehoshaphat (II Chronicles 20)

*   The Centurion (Matthew 8:10)

Chapter 12
DISCUSSION QUESTIONS

1. Discuss the differences and evidences of:
   - Saving faith

   - Persevering faith

   - Aggressive faith

2. Discuss specific ways that you have stepped out in faith and trusted God.

3. Faith is like a spiritual muscle, how can you make it stronger?

4. How can you encourage others to walk by faith?

CHAPTER 13

Steps to Walking by Faith

So how do you start walking by faith, trusting God to work through you to accomplish His work? I have summarized what I have learned over the years into the following principles.

Principle 1: To be used of God, we must be clean vessels.

After the coffeehouse closed, I prayed and waited to see where God would lead us next. Everything I did with the teenagers was with the purpose of their seeing God work. I thought doing one of the "folk musicals," which were popular at the time, would provide that opportunity. In thinking it through, I realized we needed someone to lead music, so I prayed for God to bring just the right person. Frank and I were eating dinner one night and out of the blue he said, "Honey, have you ever thought about doing one of those folk musicals?" I was shocked that he brought it up and told him of my prayer. He proceeded to tell me that a young doctor, who had previously directed musicals, had recently joined the church. The young man had indicated his interest in doing one with the Briarwood youth.

I met with the young doctor and told him of my vision of using a musical to show the kids how to pray, step out in faith, and see God work the impossible. He was very excited about the possibilities, so we gathered the kids together and presented the situation. We told them we were going to learn to pray, not making our needs known to anyone but God. They were hesitant, but willing to take the challenge. Needing two hundred dollars to buy the music, we prayed that within two weeks God would provide the money. When you step out in faith sometimes you let your needs be known, sometimes you work it out yourself, and sometimes you pray and wait. I felt like God was leading us to pray and wait. After they left, I questioned the wisdom of leading them in this step of faith. But deep down I knew God wanted them to see Him work.

A lady from the church came to me the next morning. She said she did not know what my need was right then, but as she was praying that morning, God had impressed on her to bring me the $50 she had been saving. I told her about the musical and our prayer and she agreed the money must be part of the answer. In the afternoon someone gave me a check for $45 because she was tithing her income tax refund. In the next day and a half, a total of $175 came from the most unexpected places. It was an exciting time and the kids called every 15 minutes asking me the latest on how much I had received. They were so thrilled and excited to see God at work.

On Friday night Frank and I went to a staff dinner at the church. At the end, he had all of the men go around and introduce their wives. As they went they would say things like, "This is my beautiful wife of 15 years," or "This is the sweetheart of my home." Each accolade got better and better as the men tried to out do each other. When it got back around to Frank, I was not surprised when he said, "And you know my wife, Barbara." I really had not expected much more from him because, well, Frank is just Frank. He does not say a whole lot about anything. But he went on to say, "I want to tell you about my right hand, the one I couldn't do without, the one who keeps me on track." On and on he went.

I was sitting there in shock, thinking how he never said things like that. As he continued with the accolades, I began silently communicating with the audience, "Oh, I'm really not as wonderful as all that." And the audience responded back to me with affirming nods their agreement with Frank's praise. He was oblivious to this non-verbal communication.

As he finished his little tribute he said, "My secretary, Marilyn Beard." I inwardly gasped. After making such a fool of myself in front of everyone, I thought I was going to die. They were so embarrassed for me, they would not look at me. It was the most humiliating moment of my life. (That's a little bit of an exaggeration, but you know what I mean.) I wanted to shrink under the chair and crawl out of the room. But somehow I got through the rest of the dinner and rushed out through the kitchen. Having driven my own car, I got home before Frank and went straight to bed. When he finally came into the bedroom, he said, "Honey, don't you want to pray?"

I said, "No, I'm tired."

"Are you mad at me?"

"No, I'm just sleepy."

"Well, okay."

The next morning I got up quickly and was busying around the kitchen when he came in and asked me again if I wanted to pray. I told him I was busy. Clueless, he asked if he had done anything wrong. Again I denied it using busyness as my excuse. He tried a little more to find out what was wrong, but eventually gave up and left for the church. Meantime, my heart had hardened like a stone. I was humiliated and frankly a little bit jealous. I knew I was being silly about the whole thing, but my pride would not let me admit to him my foolish actions.

Strangely, at that point, the money for the musical stopped coming. Nothing. The kids called and I had to tell them there was no change. In my heart I knew the reason — I should forgive Frank.

My breaking point came the next Wednesday when one teenager called to suggest that maybe God knew we were only going to need $175. Deep down I knew it was not true. God was not going to provide through an unclean vessel. After I hung up, I started praying about the whole situation. It was like God was asking, "Barbara, do you want to prevent the kids from seeing Me work by holding on to your sin?" I knew I could not do that.

As I was praying, I held my hand out and said, "God, my heart is hard as a rock and I'm too embarrassed to talk to Frank. But if you'll melt my heart, I will go to him and ask for his forgiveness. But first, I ask for Your forgiveness. Make me a clean vessel for Your use and don't let me block those kids' view of You." Right at that moment my heart felt like it turned to water and melted in my hand.

I got up from my knees and called Frank. Marilyn put me through immediately, which was unusual given his busy schedule. I told him the whole story and asked for his forgiveness. There was never any doubt in my mind that he would not be sweet and forgiving; it was just my pride that had held me back. While we were talking, the doorbell rang. When I went to the door, there was a lady from the church with a $25 check. She said, "I have been riding around with this money for a week intending to give it to you."

Why do you think God had her hold that check for a week? There is no doubt in my mind God was orchestrating the whole situation. It was obvious the money had been intended for me for a week, but God was waiting for me to acknowledge my sin and ask for forgiveness before He let it be delivered. We have to remember that when we hold onto our sin, we can block the working of God in our lives and thus deprive others of seeing Him work. Our sin does not only affect us; its effects ripple into the lives of others.

Principle 2: To be used of God, we have to do it His way, in His timing.

One fall the ballet was very busy working on the dance for Briarwood Church's Christmas festival and a joint performance with the Ballet Magnificat, a professional Christian ballet company out of Jackson, Mississippi. Since we were charging admission for the Ballet Magnificat performance, I wrote and asked permission to use the recording of the music to which we were dancing. In the past when I had requested permission, we either did not hear back from them or they sent us permission with a nice "thank you for asking." However, this time, with three weeks left before the performance, I received a response from Telarc Records saying they were sorry, but could not give us permission to use their music.

I called and asked the reason; after all, they had never denied us in the past. They told me their contract with the National Federation of Musicians in New York City would not allow them to license that particular recording. My heart froze. It was a huge piece involving all of the dancers, a long dance and the most important part of our program. We were all ready and it was too late to prepare a replacement piece. But my very next thought was, "God is sovereign. Am I willing to trust Him?"

The next day I gathered all of the ballet students together to pray God would work in the hearts of the leadership of the National Federation to give us permission. Trusting God, I called the Federation and explained our situation. They were not terribly interested in the spiritual impact we were trying to make in Birmingham. However, they **were** interested in the financial benefit they would be getting — and in an unfriendly way, may I add. They agreed to discuss it and get back with us. I faxed them the requested additional information.

Several times I was tempted to go ahead and use the music without their permission. After all, how would they know? But I knew I could not ask for God's blessing on something I was not doing His way.

WAITING ON GOD IN PRAYER

Pray, then wait and wait and wait . . .
God will respond – He won't be late.
He sees with eyes beyond the years,
He loves with love beyond my tears.
He knows I'm weak, I doubt, I fear . . .
He knows I do not "feel" Him near.
He watches, 'though I cannot see,
When I feel lost, He's guiding me.
When hopes may fade and dreams grow dim
With eyes of faith – just look at Him!
What once committed to His care
Through earnest and believing prayer,
Is ever on His active file
In which He's working all the while,
Perfecting that which touches me
Until His perfect will I see![1]

The time for the performance was fast approaching and the students, faculty, and I continued to pray and trust God. The Federation's response finally came:

the local musicians' union in Birmingham would need to make the decision.

The following Sunday, before the morning worship service, I saw a member of Briarwood who played in the Alabama Symphony. Members of the Symphony were there playing for the Thanksgiving service at which we were also dancing. When I asked her who the head of the local chapter of the National Federation of Musicians was, she said it was the cellist who was at that very moment on the stage with us. We had gone around the world with this request and the person who needed to give us permission was playing for our performance at Briarwood Church. Through him the local federation granted the permission we needed and, with four days to spare, we were "legal."

To be used of God you must play according to His rules – "... *if anyone competes as an athlete, he does not receive the victor's crown unless he competes according to the rules" (II Timothy 2:5).*

Principle 3: Faith comes from knowing God and His purposes as they are revealed in Scripture.

"Consequently, faith comes from hearing the message, and the message is heard through the word of Christ" (Romans 10:17).

One year was unusually demanding for the ballet school. In the fall, the Ballet Exaltation went to dance and minister in Russia; there was a Christmas performance, and then the Russians came in January for a workshop. In addition, there were two college performances, and an Easter performance. The first time I had a chance to think about the May ballet was at the beginning of April. To make it even more diffi- cult, I had written a new ballet story which would require all new music and choreography.

One morning as I sat down for my quiet time, I thought, "Lord, there is no way to get this done. If I schedule every minute of every day for the next six weeks, I still won't have enough time." As I read in John 6 about Jesus' feeding the five thousand, my mind was not engaged. I was just too overwhelmed to concentrate.

Suddenly it was like God was telling me to stop and think about what I was reading. I prayed, "Lord, there's not a lot of correlation between those loaves and fishes and what I am facing."

"Go back, Barbara, and read it again," the still, small voice spoke to my spirit.

I went back and read it more carefully and then went over to Mark 6 and read the parallel passage. Suddenly, I realized I was reading about an impos- sible situation. I was in an impossible situation. Was God trying to teach me lessons from the passage that I could apply in my present circumstance?

In the story I saw how God met their need for food when there seemed to be no source for provi- sion. As I read, very clear steps began to emerge which I related to my need with the ballet. The first thing Jesus did when confronted with an impossibility was to instruct Philip to **analyze** the situation – too many people, too little food. So step one for me was to assess my problem. That was simple; I was in an impossible situation, too much to do in too little time.

What did God teach in the story about impossible situations? "I can supply all of your needs." Okay, I got that. God had the power to do everything necessary for the ballet performance to go on. Check.

Secondly, He **organized** for the provision by instructing the disciples to divide the people into groups of tens and fifties. The application of this lesson was to go ahead and make the rehearsal schedule for that very night; even though, I did not have the music or the choreography. Done.

Thirdly, I was to **energize** by getting together what He had already supplied and use it. That afternoon, right before rehearsal, I reached into my bag of tapes, not even looking to see what I grabbed. I could tell immediately the music was perfect, with the right tempo and length with a musical interlude for the dramatic sequence which was needed. I did not even have time to work out choreography, so when the girls walked in, I just started dancing to the music. The choreography flowed out of me. What normally took hours happened in the span of a few minutes. It was God.

The final step was to **leave the results to God**. I trusted Him to work through every detail to produce a ballet which would give Him glory and draw others to Himself, which is exactly what He did. Each day I had to return to Him for that day's provision, just like the Israelites' daily provision of manna. The ballet turned out to be one of the best we ever performed. There was a lot of hard work and my faith was tested to the limit day after day, but in the end God proved Himself faithful.

Principle 4: God responds to the prayers of His people.

Prayer is an integral part of walking by faith. James 4:2c tells us that we do not have because we do not ask. Someone once said, "Prayer is God's dignifying man by giving him causality in what He is doing." It is the communication line with out Heavenly Father, Who is the source of all that is needed to live effectively for Him. God tells us in Jeremiah 33:3, *"Call to me and I will answer you and tell you great and unsearchable things you do not know."* And in James 5:16b: *"The prayer of a righteous man is powerful and effective."*

> *Prayer is God's dignifying*
> *man by giving him causality*
> *in what He is doing.*

For our spring ballet one year, we were going to perform an original story ballet, "The Heart of the Toymaker," which required two young girls to dance the leads. Finding just the right ones who could handle the difficult choreography and also act was a real challenge. After much prayer and several auditions, we found two little fourth-grade girls who were perfect.

Just as we were getting to the point of putting it all together, I received a call from the mother of one of the lead dancers. Jennifer had fallen and broken her ankle over the weekend. The doctor had put it in a cast and said he would look at it again in three weeks. When God brings opportunities of faith, I always get an initial panicky feeling. A dear friend once told me, "Barbara, you love to tell your faith stories, but you never like living them!" I was perplexed as to how to proceed with this challenge. We could not wait three weeks to see if she could dance; plus, she could not afford to lose that much time from rehearsal. It was a real blow, especially since there was no understudy. What was God going to do? There was no possible way of getting another dancer at that late date.

Two days later in my quiet time, I read in Isaiah 31 about God's rebuking the Israelites for going to Egypt to find provision. He wanted them to trust Him to meet their needs in ways they could not see. I felt God was telling me not to spend time trying to replace Jennifer. He wanted to show His power by meeting our need for a dancer in a supernatural way.

When I sense the leading to step out and trust God for something impossible, it is almost immediately followed by doubt. I question whether I am I trying to "hot-dog." Is it **my** desire for a miracle, or God's desire for me to trust Him for a miracle? But over the years I have learned not to dig up in doubt what was planted in faith, so I trust in the light I am given. And almost always God confirms the leading through Scripture during my quiet times. God's Word is instrumental in my stepping out on faith and offers the guidance as to how to pray.

> *I have learned not to dig up in doubt what was planted in faith.*

At the prayer breakfast the next Saturday morning, I asked the men to pray for God to heal Jennifer's foot. Frank, who started me on this wild journey of faith, looked over and told me I needed an understudy. I told him, "If we did that, we would be going back to Egypt (making our own provision rather than trusting God to provide). The faith you taught me doesn't have safety nets." As I was going about the house that morning, I heard the men in every room stepping out in faith, praying for God to heal her little foot.

Then the ballet joined in the prayer. My Bible study girls prayed. The word got around and all over town people asked God to glorify Himself by supernaturally healing Jennifer.

On the following Monday, a week after the first call, Jennifer went back to the doctor who examined her foot and then x-rayed it. There was no break! After removing the cast, he wrapped it in an ace bandage and told her to take it easy for a few days. Later at a party this same doctor, who was not a Christian, discussed the situation with another ballet mom and said, "Children's bones heal remarkably fast, but that was truly unusual."

Jennifer danced beautifully in the performance that spring while everyone praised God for His miracle.

The Bible instructs us to come boldly before God with our requests (Matthew 7:7-9) because He will answer (Psalm 17:6). Jesus tells us to persevere in prayer. In His parable of the persistent widow (Luke 18:1-8), He teaches us to *"pray and not give up (verse*

1)." Prayer is hard work and we can become easily discouraged and distracted, but we should never let up in bringing requests to Him.

> **Prayer is hard work and we can
> become easily discouraged and distracted.**

Principle 5: Trusting God requires a child-like faith.

When Peggy was about three years old, she told us that she wanted a white fluffy dog. We told her we just could not get a dog right then; there were too many mouths to feed as it was. Without hesitation she said, "That's okay. I'll just ask Jesus to give me a dog." From that point on she prayed morning, noon, and night. Every time someone came to our house to pray, whether it was about divorce or suicide, she would come alongside them and pray for a white fluffy dog.

Frank and I were touched by this sweet little girl's persistence, so we started looking for a dog. But there was not one to be found in the city of Birmingham, except the $150 kind, and we were not going that route. I was beginning to panic because I felt I needed to get her a dog so her faith in God would not be hindered. I had to make sure God came through in order for her to continue to trust Him — or so I thought. In reality, God was teaching me more about faith than He was teaching Peggy.

One day at the breakfast table she prayed, "Lord Jesus, I'm tired of waiting and I want my dog today."

Later that day we returned home to find a little white fluffy ball of fur in our backyard fence. Peggy walked right up to it and said, "There's my dog," with a tone that sounded like, "Lord, You sure took Your time." I wondered if the dog fell out of heaven. We took it inside, but I kept telling Peggy the dog had to belong to someone and probably was not hers.

About an hour later we got a call from the dean of women at Southeastern Bible College, who was also a member of Briarwood. She asked me if I had found the dog she left. Sally told me that six weeks previously, about the time Peggy began to pray, a student found a newborn puppy and raised it in a shoebox under her bed. This day school was out and no one could take it with them. The student brought it to Sally and asked her if she knew of anyone who could provide a good home for the dog. Sally immediately remembered hearing Peggy pray for a little white fluffy dog when Sally was at our home praying about starting Briarwood Christian School.

Frisky lived with us for 16 years before she went home to be with the Lord. (I am convinced that there are dogs in heaven!) She was always a tangible testament to the fact that God will build the faith of my children and their faith does not depend on me.

Through that story God showed me what child-like faith looks like. We are children of a very loving and compassionate God, Who desires to give good gifts to us (Matthew 7:11). Child-like faith accepts God at His word, trusting in His character, no matter how irrational or illogical that seems, without seconding guessing Him or His motives. Faith is not about what other people think and is undeterred by their skepticism. Hebrews 11:1 defines child-like faith perfectly: *"faith is being sure of what we hope for and certain of what we do not see."*

Principle 6: Walking by faith requires relying on God's strength and power.

Zechariah 4:6b summarizes a principle that we find in Scripture: *"'Not by might nor by power, but by my Spirit,' says the LORD Almighty."* *"But God chose the foolish things of the world to shame the wise; God chose the weak things of the world to shame the strong"* (I Corinthians 1:27). Why? *"So that no one may boast before him"* (1:29). *"But we have this treasure in jars of clay to show that this all-surpassing power is from God and not from us"* (II Corinthians 4:7). *"Therefore I will boast all the more gladly about my weaknesses, so that Christ's power may rest on me"* (II Corinthians 12:9b). And Jesus said in John 15:5b, *"Apart from me you can do nothing."* We cannot do anything that matters apart from God.

We fail to cooperate with His plan when we try to work out His assignments in our own power. So how do we appropriate God's strength and power? Frank uses an outline from John 15 to explain how to abide in Christ and walk in the Spirit. First we must **rely** on God and acknowledge that we have no resources in and of ourselves. Next we **retain** God's Word in our hearts. How can we rely on something that He has not promised? We have to know what God's Word says. As we study Scripture, the convicting power of the Holy Spirit shows us areas in our lives which are not consistent with His will. Then as we **relinquish** our wills to His, we are emptied to receive His power. *"Dear friends, if our hearts do not condemn us, we have confidence before God and receive from him anything we ask, because we obey his commands and do what pleases him" (I John 3:21-22).* The next step is to **request**, which goes back to what we learned in Principle 3 on prayer. Lastly, **resist** the devil. Satan cannot stand to see the power of God operating through a Christian, so he will bring an all-out assault on those that walk with God. We must learn to use the armor of God in resisting the enemy (Ephesians 6:10-20), which leads right into the next principle.

Principle 7: Leave the results to God.

When we have presented ourselves to God for His service, asked Him to cleanse us, and prayed for Him to accomplish His work through us, we must leave the results to Him, or said another way, **rest** in Him. This is the evidence that we are walking by faith and not by sight (II Corinthians 5:7).

At times I weep because I do not see God's drawing people to Himself when I speak. I want to see the fruit. But my job is to sow and cultivate. God's job is to bring the harvest. One time I spoke in Roanoke, Virginia at a large women's event. With all my heart I gave the Gospel very clearly, but after the invitation there was not one person out of the big group who indicated a decision for Christ. I just knew the ladies who asked me to speak were thinking I was a failure. I left feeling so disappointed. Later when recounting the event to Elizabeth Newbold, a great woman of faith, I said, "I'm not going to speak again. God doesn't use me. That's not what I'm supposed to be doing."

I'll never forget what she said, "Who asked you to be the fruit inspector?" She went on to say that we are simply the channels and instruments God uses and He is the One who produces the results — in His timing. I shutter to think how different the course of my life would have been if I had continued to look for results rather than to the Lord Jesus.

Elizabeth Newbold: "Who asked you to be the fruit inspector?"

It just so happened that ten years later the ladies in Roanoke asked me to speak at the same annual event. Why, I don't know. Maybe they thought I had improved. While sitting at the head table, trying to keep my focus on the fact that God would be the One speaking through me, the chairman leaned over and said to me, "This is a significant day for me. It's my first day as chairman; but more importantly, it was when you spoke ten years ago that I accepted Christ." I was overwhelmed at the goodness of God to encourage me in that way. We do not have to see what He is doing. But when we trust Him in faith to use us, we can be confident in the fact He will.

One time when Stuart Briscoe spoke at Briarwood, he said, "When one believes in Jesus, rivers of living water will flow out of his inner most being. *'Jesus*

. . . *said . . 'If anyone is thirsty, let him come to me and drink. Whoever believes in me, as the Scripture has said, streams of living water will flow from within him" (John 7:37-38).* And where the waters flow, the flowers grow." When we trust Jesus to flow through us, we may never see the flowers, but can be assured that they are there. *"But thanks be to God, who always leads un in triumphal procession in Christ and through us spreads everywhere the fragrance of knowledge of him" (II Corinthians 2:14).*

One day in church a member brought a young lady to me. The member said, "She recently became a Christian and wants to talk to a real Christian, so I brought her to you." It turned out that three years earlier, this young Jewish woman had been in Panama City, Florida and someone from our church's college outreach ministry had shared the Gospel with her using a Four Spiritual Laws booklet. At the time the Jewish lady was very put off and showed no interest whatsoever in hearing about Christ. However, for some unknown reason, she had kept the little booklet. Recently, the young woman was going through a very difficult time and decided to pull the booklet out and read it. She noticed Briarwood's name and address was stamped on the back of it and decided to come to church. On her first visit, she had prayed to receive Christ when Frank gave the invitation at the end of his sermon.

Desiring to learn more about her new-found faith, she had sought out someone. That's how we came to meet. Over the next few months she became involved with the singles' Bible study that met in our basement on Sunday nights and she grew in her walk with God by leaps and bounds. Eventually the Lord called her to reach out to other Jews by being the editor of a Messianic Jew newspaper.

We should never be discouraged when we do not see the fruit of our labors. The person on beach project who shared with that random girl had no idea that years later God would use the planted seed to bear much fruit. There is an old saying, "Anyone can count the seeds in an apple, but only God can count the apples in a seed."

Anyone can count the seeds in an apple,
but only God can count the apples in a seed.

Principle 8: Remember God's faithfulness of the past.

Many times discouragement comes when we do not understand God's purposes and timing as we see events unfold. But when we remember His past works of faithfulness, we become confident that God will work. The truth is no matter what we are **seeing**, His purposes will not be thwarted by anyone or any circumstance.

God's purposes will not be thwarted
by anyone or any circumstance.

When I am tempted to be discouraged, I often remember back to when Briarwood began a new inner-city ministry. This was in the late 1960s during those turbulent years of racial tension which, unfortunately, Birmingham is famous for. The church ran a summer camp for inner-city youth the previous year and it was very successful. We planned to expand it, but needed to raise some money. Frank organized a luncheon to present the idea and invited all the "rich friends" he knew. He and others involved were going to propose a way to reach the black community with the Gospel, along with testimonies from the previous summer, and ask the attendees for financial commitments. Any man there could have given all that we needed without even missing it, so I was very optimistic.

While the luncheon was taking place, I was home praying for God to provide through this group. When Frank got home, I asked him how much money they pledged. I was shocked when he said $500, which was not nearly enough money. I said, "Frank, what are we going to do? Those were the only rich people we know. Who do we have left?"

Frank said, "You're right, honey. Now all we have left is God."

In various ways the needed money eventually came in, along with just the right people to lead the ministry. A separate book needs to be written recounting all of the lives that God has changed, and continues to change, through that ministry and the ministries that were started from it.

Principle 9: Remember why we walk by faith: to put the spotlight on God.

What is God's purpose in using us? The fact is that He doesn't need us; He could cause the stones to cry out or speak through donkeys. But for some reason He ordained that the means He would use to accomplish His purposes would be weak and fallible men and women. Why did He choose insufficient instruments for such impossible tasks? The answer is very simple: so that all will see Him and not us.

So whenever I am tempted to be discouraged, I think back on stories like these and the lessons I have learned. I am confident that if God calls me to a task, He will bring every resource necessary to see it completed. He has never failed. Great is His faithfulness!

BEING USED

O Father God, my sinful heart is full
So humbled and amazed with grace I stand
Ashamed for judgments made for lack of faith
To see the greatness of Your sovereign hand.

But wonder now I feel for Who You are
To use such weak and sinful men as we
To finish that which You began to do
To build Your kingdom and set the captives free.

In human pride I felt You should rely
On wisdom and the power that resides in men.
I only saw the polished vessels of our worth
As useful to convict the world of sin.

But, Lord, Your grace has overwhelmed my pride.
I see Your plan to use the foolish and the weak
To demonstrate to all the glory of Your will
And through our feeble efforts save the meek.

But why, O mighty wise and holy God,
Would You entrust Your work
To feeble fools like me
When angels stand on tiptoes just to know
And do Your bidding perfectly.

So gratefully I bow in wonder, love, and awe
And offer now my feeble strength to You
To show the world Your wisdom and Your grace
To do Your glorious work through
whom You choose.

My only plea now, gracious Lord and friend,
Is that I for one may ever faithful be
To believe that You will do mighty works
Through simple just believing souls like me.

And keeping eyes of faith fixed on
Your glorious face
May know in truth divine enablement
And step out on the waters of the raging sea
Trusting, hoping, willing, and obedient.[2]

MY PRAYER

Dear Lord, I want to be used as Your instrument
to impact the world for You. To do this I must be

willing to go outside my comfort zone and trust You to work the impossible through me. Give me courage, strength, power, and patience. And may the spotlight always be on You and not me. In Your powerful name, amen.

Notes

[1] Barker, Barbara B.

[2] Ibid.

Chapter 13
PERSONAL APPLICATION

1. Have you ever asked God to show you anything that displeases Him? What was the result?

2. Is there an area of your life that you are not giving God total control?

3. In what ways are you limiting God in working through you?

Chapter 13
BIBLE STUDY

God uses clean vessels. What are the steps to clean your vessel?

- Psalm 139:23-24

- I John 1:9

Prayer is a very integral part of walking by faith. What do you learn about prayer from the following verses?

- Romans 8:26-27

- Matthew 7:7

- Luke 18:1

- Ezra 8:23

- James 4:2-3

- II Chronicles 7:14

- Mark 11:24

- James 5:16, I John 3:22

Walking in faith means that you rely on God to give you strength and direct your steps, trusting His Holy Spirit to work through you. The Greek word for filled, "*pleroo*," literally means "to be characterized by." What do the following verses teach you about being filled, or characterized, by the Holy Spirit?

- Ephesians 5:18

- Acts 7:55

- Acts 11:24

- Acts 13:52

Write Luke 18:27 in your own words.

Many times we limit God's work in us and through us by perceiving God as small. Mother Angelica once said, "When I think of God, I've learned to think big." What do you learn about God from the following verses?

- I Chronicles 29:12

- II Chronicles 25:8

- Ephesians 3:20

Chapter 13
DISCUSSION QUESTIONS

1. If stepping out in radical faith is your goal, what do you need to change in your prayer life?

2. What impossible situation is God prompting you to step out in faith and trust Him?

3. Look back in your life and recount the times God came through.

4. How will remembering those times help you walk in faith in the future?

CHAPTER 14

Faithful to the Finish

Probably the biggest test to my faith in recent years came when Frank decided to step down as senior pastor of Briarwood. Many factors entered into his decision, but the primary motivation was his desire to ensure a smooth transition. He realized as he got older he could be at a higher risk for developing a life-threatening illness. If something suddenly happened to him, the church would suffer. He had prayed about his retirement long before he announced it to me or the world, so during that time, he had a chance to internalize and adjust to the change. However, when he told me of his intentions, I was caught off guard and a floodgate of emotions burst forth.

I was aware that all I had known for forty years was about to change dramatically and my heart nearly broke in two. I would no longer be the "pastor's wife." When I had married Frank the church was meeting in a little storefront building. Over the years we had nurtured it, watched it grow, and with a death grip held it together when the enemy tried to rip it apart. My children were on staff and my ballet ministry was based there. The whole family ministered together. If the retirement was not a big enough blow, my daughter, Anita, and her husband, Billy, announced they were moving to Arizona to plant a church. (And they had the nerve to tell me that they were taking my grandchildren with them!) To top it all off, Missy, my little dog for sixteen years, died. I felt stripped to my very core.

Briarwood went through a relatively short search process and with a 100% vote of support from the congregation, a new man came to lead our beloved flock, bringing along another "pastor's wife." Don't get me wrong, we love Harry and Cindy Reeder and believe that they are God's provision for Briarwood. And we are very grateful for Harry's graciousness in asking Frank to assume the position of pastor emeritus and allowing us to stay at Briarwood. But the transition was hard for me.

In the months leading up to Frank's announcement, I had been asking the Lord to show me if the motivation behind my ministry was pure. Was I building God's kingdom or the kingdom of Briarwood? Like the psalmist, I prayed: *"Search me, O God, and know my heart; test me and know my anxious thoughts. See if there is any offensive way in me, and lead me in the way" (Psalm 139:23-24).* God is always concerned with matters of the heart, so it did not take long for Him to show me my true motivations — and they weren't pretty.

BLIND SPOTS

Blind spot – do I have one?
A place I do not see my sin;
While feeling outwardly okay
Is there a hidden place somewhere within
Where lurks an "enemy in the camp"
That blocks the way for others to see HIM?

Blind spots – in others seen so well
As I observe them from the outside in,
And judge their hearts, 'tho not convicted yet,
And pride myself on how I "might have been"
Had I been in the place where they now are –
While my own faults I easily defend.

Blind spots – what a hypocrite I am!
To know my heart how should I now begin?
O, will You search me gently, Lord –
And try my heart, and to Your own heart bend;
And break me, if You must – I trust Your hand;
Just let my faith be real and not pretend![1]

As I said before, with Frank's announcement God revealed sins of pride, jealousy, anxiousness, and insecurity, to name a few. My sin made me sick. But what could I do with all of these thoughts and feelings that seemed so overwhelming? More than anything I wanted my heart to be right before the Lord, but how could I go about changing my heart?

CHANGE MY HEART, O GOD!

How long does it take to change a heart?
Does my will and obedience play a part?
Where lies the line between spirit and flesh?
What part is effort – what part is grace?
When do we speak of what is not "felt"?
How can one "will" for his cold heart to melt?

Oh, to be blameless, sincere in my faith –
Faithfully running my God-ordained race.

How does one change what his flesh is desiring?
How does one hate what his heart is admiring?
How does one focus on things up above –
When it's things here on earth that his spirit loves?
Can one determine by sheer will to be
A Christian example for others to see?
When wars of the flesh are raging inside
With coveting, jealousy, anger, and pride?
And, yet, to allow "hidden things" to be seen –
Would prove unacceptable – and I'm caught
in between.
Hypocrisy, as ugly as this word may be,
Is better than showing the sin that's in me.

So what? Shall I hide behind a face that's not real?
Or hide *ME* – so that no one can know how I feel?

I know. The answer is *"trust and obey,"*
And that's what I long for with every new day.
My comfort is knowing I'd *have* no "conviction" –
If Your Spirit and Word had not given descriptions

Of what *You* have purposed to do in my life –
(For You're not the author of confusion and strife.)
That it's You Who is showing this state
of my heart –
My conception in sinfulness right from the start,
That my souls' greatest Enemy would
keep me so low
That Your power and Your victory I
never would know.

So, I'll reach out to trust that this war You will win
–
And someday remove all this burden of sin.
That someday, in *this* world – 'twill be *YOU*
and not *I* –
And the "me" that resists will finally die;
And Your grace in my life will be on display –
To the praise of the glory of Your wise holy ways.[2]

During this time, I studied Scripture as if it were
a life preserver thrown to a drowning person – which,
of course, it was – and several principles became
very clear to me. First of all, the heart is deceitful
(Jeremiah 17:9). When we become Christians, God
gives us a new heart, but our sinful nature still resides
within us. From the moment of conversion until the
time we die we are works in progress as we gradually
become more like Christ (Romans 8:29).

Secondly, God commands us to put on the new
nature and put off the old sinful one. As we feed and
nurture the new heart, or spiritual nature, it becomes

stronger and more in control, and the sinful nature becomes weaker and less in control.

Thirdly, we can rely on God's promises to answer our prayers for a new heart in this matter. I Thessalonians 5:24 tells us, *"The one who calls you is faithful and he will do it."* And Jesus said in Mark 11:24 says, *"Therefore, I tell you, whatever you ask for in prayer, believe that you have received it, and it will be yours."*

Lastly, the longer we look into our hearts, the more discouraged we will be. But as we look to Him, the Author and Perfecter of our faith (Hebrews 12:2), we will be transformed (Romans 12:2). *"But we all, with open face beholding as in a glass the glory of the Lord, are changed into the same image from glory to glory, even as by the Spirit of the Lord"* (II Corinthians 3:18, KJV).

I still get a little jab when someone introduces our pastor and his wife and realize they are not speaking of Frank and me, but I know that God loves me and He has me exactly where He wants me. More than anything else I want to appropriate God's power in my daily life and be used in the lives of others. Paul teaches us that this involves sharing in Christ's suffering, which means dying to self. *"I want to know Christ and the power of his resurrection and the fellowship of sharing in his suffering"* (Philippians 3:10).

THE LAST SUNDAY

This is the last day he'll stand before his people
Beneath the towering spire of Briarwood's
mighty steeple,
The Pastor of a flock well fed
A faithful shepherd in Christ's stead.

The people hear, "The Spirit gives them life."
They rise in bold obedience to enter in the fight.

One vision he has followed,
with steady pace and sure
One message he has taught us –
the Gospel sweet and pure.
The life he's lived before us revealed
His Father's love,
Denying self - applying grace with wisdom
from above,
He's taught the Word in depth, with heart,
And lived its truth before us.
We've watched him walk through stormy times
With courage and unwavering trust,
- unfinished [3]

A few years ago, after seeing several great
Christians fall into sinful lifestyles and turn their
backs on God, I went through an intense searching
time, asking the Lord, "How do I know that I will
not fall away from the faith? How can I be sure that
my heart will never grow cold toward You?" More
than anything, I wanted — and still do — to stay
faithful to the finish and hear those words from the

Lord Jesus, *"Well done, good and faithful servant"* *(Matthew 25:21).*

Through this process, I came to realize that succumbing to sin does not happen overnight and it always begins with small compromises of faith. Therefore, I must take a very active role in guarding my heart from the enemies of the faith – the world, my own sinful nature, and the devil himself.

There is a real and ever present adversary of our faith that seeks to steal, kill, and destroy (John 10:10a). He delights in nothing more than to see us fail. The devil is a very active "tempter" and will go to great lengths to create stumbling blocks for our faith.

Discouragement is one of Satan's most widely used weapons. Somewhere along the way I came across this allegorical story on discouragement:

It was announced that the devil was going out of business and would sell his equipment to those who would pay the price. On the day of the sale all of his tools were attractively displayed, if 'attractive' is the proper word to use. There were envy, jealousy, hatred, pride, deceit, sensuality, malice, idolatry, and many other implements of evil on display, each marked with its price.

Off by itself in a glass case was a harmless looking wedge-shaped tool, very worn, but priced higher than any other tool. Someone asked the devil what it was. "That is discouragement," he said. "And why have you priced it so high?" "Because," replied the devil, "It is more useful to me than any of the others. I can pry open and get inside a man's heart with that when I could not get near him with any of the other tools. Once inside, I can use him in whatever way suits me best. It is worn because I use it on everybody, and few know it belongs to me."

Much more could be written about the devil's tactics, but suffice it say that he is out there like a ruthless roaring lion ready to pounce (I Peter 5:8).

People in our society who do not acknowledge God bombard us with all kinds of temptations. Music, television, and movies rapidly fire messages that are contrary to the truths taught in the Bible. Not only that, but mainstream media mocks the very faith that we are trying to embrace. "Non-Christians" who most vehemently espouse tolerance are surprisingly intolerant of anything "Christian."

We must not forget that another powerful enemy to faith is our own sinful nature, which can block the Holy Spirit's ability to work in and through us. Sinful desires for pleasure, comfort, and recognition can hinder us from discerning God's will. Hard times, and the discouragement that often comes with them, can weigh us down. Unrealistic expectations of God and others set us up for certain disappointment. When we do not forgive others, bitterness can take root in our souls. And, of course, pride, the mother of all sins, is very destructive.

We are more susceptible to the attacks from without and within when our hearts have grown cold and we have lost our passion for the Lord. How does this happen? When I thought about this, I concluded that hearts grow cold in little tiny increments, by slowly, but consistently drifting away from the things that were once real and precious. When we begin to neglect our personal time with the Lord, our faith becomes weaker. It can be so subtle that we really do not notice it. We become angry and impatient at little things that never seemed to bother us before, making excuses like: "I'm just tired." "It's just my hormones." And of course, "It's someone else's fault."

During this time of reflection, the verses in Psalm 71 really struck me and as a result will be my heart's prayer until the day I die. Beginning in verse 14, *"But as for me, I will always have hope; I will praise you more and more. My mouth will tell of your righteousness, of your salvation all day long, though I know not its measure. I will come and proclaim your mighty acts, O Sovereign Lord; I will proclaim your righteousness, yours alone. Since my youth, O God, you have taught me, and to this day I declare your marvelous deeds. Even when I am old and gray, do not forsake me, O God, till I declare your power to the next generation, your might to all who are to come."* I learned from these verses that if every day when I get up, I set the course of my life on these truths, day after day, then before I know it, I will see Jesus.

Each of us face, or will face, seemingly insurmountable obstacles. But just like the spies who scouted the Promised Land (Numbers 13), we have to **choose** to focus on God and trust Him to be true to His promises. We must **purpose** to look to His Word no matter what we see or feel. We cannot allow what we feel to control us, but we must fix our eyes on Jesus who is sitting beside the throne of God. Lastly, we **praise** and **thank** Him continually no matter what.

When Frank was in the Navy, he was a photo pilot for his squadron. His job was to fly at a high altitude without lights and, when he reached the intended strike target, dive straight down and take pictures. Seconds later, he would pull straight up and return to the ship. By the time he finished, he had pulled so many "Gs" that he was very disoriented. Everything in him told him he was diving when in reality he was flying a straight course. He wanted so badly to respond to his feelings, but he knew he had to trust what his instruments were showing. The temptation was so great he would grip the stick with one hand and hold it in place with other hand, fixing his eyes on the only thing he knew to be true, the instrument panel. This story illustrates how to walk by faith and not by feelings. If we respond to what we **feel** to be right, then we will get off course and experience disastrous consequences. Instead, we have to keep our eyes on the only things we know to be true – Jesus and the Bible – and at the same time holding steady to the right course with all we have.

Therefore, in the ups and downs and challenges of life, the key to remaining faithful to God is moment by moment surrendering to Him, relying on His strength, and obeying His Word. And as we cling to Him, His grip on us is even more sure. The same hand that was nailed to the cross two thousand years ago is the same hand that now grips us firmly lest we fall. We rely on His promises that He will never allow any temptation to overtake us (I Corinthians 10:13), nor will He let anyone or anything separate us from His love (Romans 8:35-39).

So how do we explain those "Christians" who turn their backs on God? Frank has a saying: "Faith that falters before the finish was faulty from the first." Given God's precious promises to us which say that those who are truly His endure to the end, the only possible explanation is the ones who fall away and never return to the faith were never His from the beginning. Jesus told a parable about seed sown in various locations, some of which grew for a time, but eventually became choked by weeds. He goes on to explain that the seed represents God's Word and the seed sown among thorns stands for those who hear, but do not reach maturity because of the distractions of life. True Christians are those who hear the Word, retain it, and persevere to produce fruit (Luke 8:4-15).

> *Frank: "Faith that falters before the finish was faulty from the first."*

Several years have gone by since "the transition" and each year gets a little easier. Even though I go through emotional periods, the dark days are over. Frank and I have settled into our new routine. He travels a good bit speaking and I often get to accompany him – which I love to do. My days are still filled with the ballet, teaching Bible studies, speaking at women's retreats, and my new love—volunteering at an inner city Christian school. Every morning I get up extremely thankful for the life He has given me and the opportunity to serve Him for one more day. I want to end with Steve Green's song which expresses my heart.

FIND US FAITHFUL

We're pilgrims on the journey of the narrow road
And those who've gone before us line the way
Cheering on the faithful, encouraging the weary,
Their lives a stirring testament of
God's sustaining grace.

Surrounded by so great a cloud of witnesses
Let us run the race not only for the prize.
But as those who've gone before us
The heritage of faithfulness passed
on through Godly lives.

After all our hopes and dreams
have come and gone.
And our children sift through all we've left behind.
May the clues that they discover and
the memories they uncover,
Become the light that leads them to the road
we each must find.

CHORUS:
Oh may all who come behind us find us faithful.
May the fire of our devotion light their way,
May the footprints that we leave lead them
to believe,
And the lives we live inspire them to obey.
Oh, may all who come behind us find us faithful.[4]

MY PRAYER

Dear Lord, I want to be faithful to the finish and hear You say, "Well, done My good and faithful servant." Please give me the strength to resist the devil and flee temptation. Alert me when I am compromising my relationship with You in the small and seemingly insignificant ways. Show me how I can encourage others to be faithful. I cannot wait to see You face to face and spend eternity with You. Amen.

Notes:

[1] Barker, Barbara B.

[2] Ibid.

[3] Ibid.

[4] Green, Steve, http://www.stlyrics.com/songs/s/stevegreen 21959/findusfaithful567183.html (accessed 12-28-06).

Chapter 14
PERSONAL APPLICATION

1. Has your heart toward spiritual things ever grown cold? Why?

2. Which enemy do you find the most difficult to overcome, the devil, the world, or your sinful nature?

3. Have you done a real "gut check" lately on your ministry motives?

Chapter 14
BIBLE STUDY

Where did Abraham consider his true home to be (Hebrews 11:9-10)?

When you die what happens?
- II Corinthians 5:1

- Luke 23:43

What did Jesus tell us about heaven?
- John 14:2

- Matthew 6:20

What is heaven like?
- Revelation 5:11

- Revelation 19:6

- Revelation 7:9

- Acts 7:55-56

- Luke 20:35-36

- II Timothy 4:8

What will the new heavens and earth be like?
- Revelation 21:1-4

- Revelation 21:7

- Revelation 21:22-27

- Revelation 22:12

- Philippians 3:21

- I Peter 5:4

- I John 3:2

Why study about the future to come?
- Romans 8:18

- II Corinthians 4:17

- I John 3:3

Chapter 14
DISCUSSION QUESTIONS

1. How can you know when your ministry motives are not right?

2. When prospects of heaven seem so glorious, why do you think Christians despair when faced with death and cling so desperately to this life?

3. Discuss what you perceive heaven to be like. Use Scripture to substantiate your answers.

HEAVENLY PERSPECTIVE

Death – O glorious rest
Of all of life the best.
The entrance into heaven's bliss –
Oh, naught of life compares with this.
'Twas for this day life was begun
'Twas for this prize the race was run.

O Christian, do not fear the grave
From sting of death He came save.
Welcome now this celebration,
The day of promised jubilation
When we shall stand before His throne
And hear the Lord say, "Welcome home!"
To join with those who've gone before
To praise Him Whom we all adore.
This garment shell of mortal flesh
Is shed – replaced by glorious dress.
Now occupied that mansion bright
Where dark and shadows yield to light!
Where hope is substance – faith is sight,
Where suffered wrongs will be made right.

. . . Yet as for now we do not know
The appointed hour for us to go.
So, Lord, allow us while we wait
In all we do to estimate
The value from Your Heavenly view
Of all we say and all we do.
What part of life will matter more
As we look back from "yonder shore"?

What of our lives will stand the test –
What is "good," but not he "best"?
What will last and what will burn?
O teach us now how to discern
So when that glorious day is here
And You have come to draw us near,
The investment of our lives will be
An honor and a praise to Thee.
And You can say to us, "Well done –
The prize is Yours – the Victory's won!"
— Barbara Barker

APPENDIX 1

BARBARA'S TESTIMONY

I grew up in Birmingham, Alabama, in a wonderful, wonderful home, a churched family that attended the Episcopal Church. My mother and father were good parents who served the Lord and taught us to respect God and be grateful for all that He did. But somehow I missed the truth of the Gospel and lived my life based on a works philosophy. I believed that God would bless me because I was good. Since my one motivating desire was to excel in ballet, I tried to be a good person so God would bless me there. In my mind, my career was dependent on God's blessing and God's blessing was dependent on how good I could be. As a result I was a real goody-goody and He did bless my dancing. From age 11 and all the way through high school I poured myself into this one pursuit, even dancing the lead for the Birmingham Ballet.

After high school, I was awarded a scholarship to a ballet school in Chicago where I attended

Northwestern University, dancing with a performing ensemble there. At the end of my freshman year I had the opportunity to tour with the group, but my daddy thought I was getting a little too full of myself. He insisted that I come back home for the summer; even though, I thought dancing in Birmingham was beneath me.

While at home I received a letter from a young man whom I grew up with in Birmingham. When I was in seventh grade, he was a senior and a life-guard at the Birmingham Country Club. I remember sitting around the pool listening to the older girls talk about him, telling all of these wild tales. He was a really bad boy. I thought, "Good girls like me would never go out with wild boys like him." Yet the years passed and I would see him at parties and other events around town, watching him from a distance. I don't even think he knew my name. He had finished Auburn University and this particular summer was in Pensacola, attending Navy flight training. He was coming home for the weekend and had written asking me to go out with him. It was at that moment that I realized why good girls like me didn't go out with bad boys like him – they don't ask us. Because once he did ask, I was really eager to go. I was surprised at how eager I was. Well, anyway, I said yes and we went out.

He was just as bad as I had heard. And I was fasci-nated. That night we went dancing at a very popular place for young people and he was inebriated, to say it politely. As we were on the dance floor later in the evening, he leaned over and whispered into my ear that I was the girl he was going to marry. I thought that was the kind of thing that boys like that say to girls like me at times like those, so I wasn't going to pay any attention to it. But I did and thought about it all week after he left.

The next Wednesday I received a letter from him that said he really meant what he said. He loved me and wanted me to be his wife someday. And more than anything, he wanted to hear from me that I loved him too. I wrote him back and told him that I was flattered, but I had plans to dance and wanted to fulfill my dreams in that area. And besides, before I told anyone I loved him I would have to think about it a really long time and be very sure. To say the least, I was preoccupied that whole week thinking about him.

When he came back the next weekend, I had thought about it a really long time (a week), so I told him that something very drastic had happened to me and I did love him and wanted to be his wife. Of course that scared him to death and he said I would have to finish college first.

After that summer I went back to Northwestern and my dancing commitments there. But for the "joy set before me" (marrying him), I finished the next three years of my college in two. Right after graduation I flew out to the West Coast to meet his aircraft carrier, which was coming in from Korea. The Frank that got off that ship was very different from the Frank that had left eight months earlier. His language was improved and he had quit drinking. He was much more serious and even talked about God some. What really disturbed me was that he no longer talked about marriage. He said that before he even thought about getting married he needed to get out of the Navy. So I left and went to Houston, Texas where I was around a lot of exciting people. But the only thing that really excited me was receiving his letters and the few times we got together.

After much anticipation, the time came for him to get out of the Navy and he planned to come see me in Houston right after his discharge. I was ready to quit everything to marry him, but, instead, I was in for a great shock. He said we couldn't get married because he was going to seminary and be a preacher! Something was terribly wrong. The only explanation I could think of was that in flying those jets off aircraft carriers, he had gotten really scared and had made some kind of crazy bargain with God. If I could just be patient, when he got to seminary he would realize that he had none of the qualities that would qualify him to be a preacher.

Knowing that it wouldn't take him long to realize that the seminary thing was all a mistake, I went back to Birmingham and danced with Town and Gown, teaching junior high school during the day. But after six months in seminary he told me that we were never going to marry. While in the Navy he had come to a sincere repentance toward God and felt the only way to balance the "bad" in his life was to go all the way in the other direction and be a preacher. In seminary he began digging into the Bible and realized that there was more to being a Christian than affirming the right things about God. He found that there is a supernatural, personal relationship with Him available to us. It is something living and vital and literally turns people's lives upside down. He learned enough to know that he didn't have this kind of relationship with God, so he was determined to eliminate everything in his life that would hinder him from devoting himself completely to the Lord. So he got rid of me.

At that point my world fell apart totally and completely. While I was still dancing, the career I had once dreamed of was no longer a possibility. The professional momentum was gone. I had invested my life in two things, dancing and this bad Navy pilot, and now they were both gone. I kept thinking that I was in a really bad dream.

The first thing I did was shake my fist in God's face. I had been so good; how could He have let this happen to me? Even in college when no one went to church, I got up and went. I didn't understand what they were saying, but I was there. And even more difficult, I had kept a morally clean slate with that bad, bad boy. Life no longer had any meaning for me with the two most important things gone. I thought I had no alternative but to end it all.

My grandfather, who was an atheist, had believed that when you die you are just "absorbed into the primal essence of life." That didn't sound so bad right then. Being too "chicken" about guns and knives and such, pills seemed like a good way to make all my problems go away. Unfortunately, my family was really healthy; the strongest thing we had in the medicine cabinet was aspirin. So I took a whole, new bottle, cursed God, and lay down on my bed waiting to be absorbed.

The next morning I woke up perfectly fine except that I had splotches all over my face. My Mama came in and said, "Barbara, you have the measles!" She took me to the doctor, who confirmed her diagnosis. He sent me home to recuperate for a week in a darkened room. But I knew it wasn't measles; obviously, something had intervened.

I knew that God had supernaturally spared me, which was a very humbling realization. During that week, I lay in bed and thought about my life. My older sister, Anita, who had been a Christian for years, would come and talk to me. When I was a teenager, she was one of those legalistic Christians, crying over the fact that I was going to hell because I was a dancer. That had really turned me off. The "religion" she practiced did not seem to bring joy in her life, so I had no desire to have anything to do with what she had. All she did was go to these Bible studies with little old ladies or girls whom I did not consider "in."

However, over the years she experienced a real transformation in her Christian life and came to know the freedom and joy of Jesus. She sat there on my bed and told me she had prayed for years that I would come to the end of my own self-sufficiency and see my need for Him. What did she mean by that? I had gone to church all my life. Then she actually implied that I was a sinner. Now that was a blow and I resented it. She obviously did not know what sin was. She hadn't been exposed to the things I had experienced in the dance world and among those "bad Navy pilots." I was pure in comparison. She was just living in a sheltered environment and didn't know what real sin was. But very lovingly she took me to the Scriptures where in I John 3:4b it says that *"sin is transgression of the Law."* And then she showed me Matthew 23:37-40 where God's Law was defined by Christ as *"loving God with all of our heart, mind, and strength and our neighbor as ourselves."* Maybe I measured up pretty well with the people I'd been around, but compared to God's standard I fell terribly short.

In one afternoon I went from the height of self-righteousness to the depth of being a sinner headed for hell. As moral and churchy as I thought I was, I was what the Bible calls a wicked, undone sinner. In God's eyes all my righteousness was as "filthy rags." Never before understanding the concept of judgment or hell, its reality was very clear in the Scriptures and, at that point, it was my destination. Then she left.

My sister was very wise to leave me there. So many times we don't appreciate the grace of God because we don't see the hopeless state that our sin has put us in. The reality is that we deserve nothing but death and separation from God and are powerless to change that fact.

Anita returned the next day with the amazing story of God's unconditional love for me and His provision of forgiveness through His Son Jesus Christ. She said that for me to be reconciled to God, I needed to put my trust and hope of salvation in the sacrificial death of Jesus. All I had to do was acknowledge what He did for me on the Cross, receive Him as my Savior, and commit my life to Him. After that long night of looking death and hell squarely in the face, that was the best news I could ever hear. I wanted the gift so badly, but I was terrified of the cost. I wasn't sure if I was ready to trust God completely with my life. What if He wanted me to go to Africa? I would have to think about such a surrender a little bit more.

The next morning the truth of Romans 8:32 came to me. Even though I didn't know that verse at the time, its logic was clear. It says, *"He who did not spare his own Son, but gave him up for us all— how will he not also, along with him, graciously give us all things?"* Doesn't it make sense that if He freely gave His own Son, paying the ultimate cost, He would surely meet all my other needs? With that thought I got down on my knees and asked Him to come into my life, surrendering all I knew of myself into His open arms. My fleshy heart was still shattered into a million pieces and my future was an uncertain maze, but I had a confidence and assurance that I had Jesus and He was enough. Everything else was going to be okay.

After my miraculous recovery from "the measles," those Bible studies my sister attended with all of the "little old ladies" and the "uncool" girls became my lifeline. Suddenly, they were the most beautiful, attractive people in the world to me. I went anywhere and everywhere there were Christians studying the Bible or praying. I lived vicariously through others' experiences of trusting God, leaning on them to tell me what the Bible said and pray for me. But God saved me for something much better than that.

Jesus soon led me out of the security of the Bible Belt to the West Coast where I lived and worked among people that had no idea of what it meant to be a Christian. When I went to church to be encouraged in my new faith, the preachers told me that I was in a "new stage of self-realization." They didn't even seem to know Jesus. When I talked to the people I danced with about Him, they would just say, "Oh, she's from the Bible Belt." Spiritually cutoff and not knowing how to pray or study the Bible for myself, I felt very out touch with God.

One night in desperation I fell on my knees in my apartment and said, "God, you have to help me. I can't do it alone." Suddenly I felt as if He was standing right behind me saying, *"Come to me, all you who are weary and burdened, and I will give you rest" (Matthew 11:28).* It was an incredibly new awareness of God's availability to me in prayer. Also, about that time I came to know that He had already sent me a teacher, the Holy Spirit. And then one day I stumbled across a little book, *What the Bible is All About* by Henrietta Meers, which helped me tremendously. It opened up the truths of the Bible book by book. During the next several years, I learned that His love and my fellowship with Him were not dependent on other people.

I led a young Danish model in my apartment complex to the Lord. My method of evangelism at that point was very simplistic. I asked her if she knew that she was a sinner going to hell. She said she did not know. Then I asked her if she wanted to go to heaven and she said she did. We began studying the Bible together, which was equally primitive. She would read a verse and I would read a verse and we then talked about what they said. This was not a very orthodox means of Bible study, but it was sufficient at the time for us to grow. God brought several other Christians along and together we learned more about His Word and how to apply it to our everyday lives.

After a few years, I started thinking that, because I was so spiritually effective, God must want me to go to Bible college. So I moved back to Birmingham and began the application process. However, every one of them turned me down, saying that dancing was not a good background for a Bible school student. I tried to explain to them that the dancing I had done wasn't provocative, but was truly a gracious art form.

One day I was filling out a follow-up application to Moody Bible College when my mother came to the door and told me I had a telephone call. Time seemed to slow down and my heart stopped beating. Somehow I knew who it was. I answered the phone and sure enough it was that bad Navy pilot who had broken up with me four years earlier so he could attend seminary and work his way to heaven. Through the sharing of an Air Force chaplain, he had come to understand that what he was working so hard to do, Christ had already accomplished for him. He had put his trust in Jesus' finished work on the Cross as his hope of salvation. He was back in Birmingham starting a church in a storefront on the outskirts of Birmingham. Hearing that I was back in town, he called to see if I wanted to go get coffee with him.

That was probably one of the most exciting nights of my life. We talked and talked, trying to catch each other up on the past four years. At 12:15 a.m., he reached over and grabbed my hand. I thought the butterflies in my stomach would fly out my ears. He said, "Barbara, why do you think that God has saved us for each other and brought us both back to Birmingham?"

I wanted to shout, "I don't know, but marry me tonight before you change your mind again." Instead, what came out of my mouth was, "I don't know, but until I know what God wants to do, I won't go one step further." That was a miracle. I realized then that God had worked very deeply in my life in that I wasn't willing to compromise my relationship with Him, even for a relationship with Frank.

Over the weeks that followed, we prayed and waited and eventually became convinced that God indeed had brought us together for His purpose. I became Mrs. Frank M. Barker, Jr. on November 3, 1961, to the horror of my mother and his, in that little storefront church.

It was a beautiful wedding. My mother transformed the concrete block room into a lovely chapel. As we recessed out of the "church" following the ceremony, the room was transformed again into a gorgeous reception hall.

Because Frank's friends married before he was a Christian and he did horrible things to them at their weddings, he was sure they would try to get back at him. He made these elaborate "Auburn engineer" getaway plans so we could leave unscathed from the church. When it came time for the car to sweep us away, Frank began to subtly maneuver me toward the door. Just at the moment the car arrived, my sister, Anita, tried to hug me goodbye. Frank shoved her out of the way and pushed me into the car. As he did, she slipped a little piece of paper in my hand. To Frank's disappointment, our dramatic exit was without chase and he sulked half way to Montgomery. His friends didn't know what to do with a preacher.

We were an hour out of town before I realized I had this note from my sister. You see, when you finally have the man you have loved for eight years, you aren't interested in more "letters from your sister." As I opened the note I saw that she had written Matthew 6:33, *"But seek first his kingdom and his righteousness and all these things will be given to you."* We pulled off the highway right then and asked God to let that be the story of our lives.

That was a glorious beginning and it lasted a week.

After waiting for Frank for eight years, I was so excited to finally be his wife. I thought he would meet all of my needs. He would make me happy, make me feel secure, and adore me. But he didn't do any of those things. I grew up in a home where my Daddy pampered my Mother, so this is what I expected of Frank. He was nothing like my father; just holding hands in public was major for him. My disappointment was crushing. To add to my insecurity, we had three babies in two and a half years and I had never babysat, nor changed a diaper.

Frank was trying to grow and pastor this new church and it seemed like everything was more important to him than me. I tried very hard to find my place, but there wasn't much of a demand for a dancing preacher's wife, which was all I was qualified to do. Playing the piano was the primary prerequisite of a wife of a minister, or so I thought, and I couldn't even do that. They did not ask me to teach Sunday School because, I suppose, they thought my "theology" was not clear. Frank wanted people to come over to our house for dinner, but I couldn't cook. All of my life I had been onstage, needing the applause it brought, and now I couldn't do anything.

During this time, I became sick with the mumps and developed more severe complications. The doctors wanted to put me in the hospital, but there wasn't a bed available. On Wednesday night I told Frank I really needed him to stay home from church visitation to take care of me and the children. But he said he had told God that he would never let anything keep him away from evangelism. You see, Satan had been throwing all of these obstacles in his way to keep him from going out. Then I told him if he walked out that door, I wouldn't be there when he got home. Obviously, it was an empty threat because I couldn't even get out of bed. His reply was, "That's between you and God." If I had had the strength I would have thrown something at him. He left and I wanted to kill him. I didn't know until later that it hurt him as much as it hurt me. About ten minutes after he left, Howard and Dixie Borland were at the back door, seeing what they could do for me. Frank was so burdened by the time he got to the church, that he had sent them to help. My needs were taken care of, but I was still angry with Frank.

In those early years, Frank was wrong in the way he compromised his responsibilities as a husband

and father. But his heart was always so bent toward the Lord, that if God had opened his eyes to his mistakes, he would have changed. I know now that God purposely kept Frank's eyes closed until He could do the work that was necessary in me. Not seeing God's master plan, I became bitter and angry and a pitiful martyr. I would put on my "preacher's wife face" and go to the church and tell people, "God bless you. Praise the Lord." That's when my drama training finally came in handy. While I put up a good front for the outside world, Frank and the children knew the real me.

One day as I was walking down the hall at Briarwood, I heard two ladies say as I passed, "Frank's wife is so sweet." Wonder what they would have thought of me if they knew I hated every one of them? My only joy in life was for Frank to come home so I could let him have it. He'd walk in the house at night and I would start in on him. "You're a horrible husband and a horrible father. Why did you ever marry me? I would leave you if it wouldn't embarrass you in front of that church." Needless to say, he was pretty miserable too and dreaded coming home. Later he said that he drove home with knots in his stomach, wishing he could go anywhere except back to me.

Ladies, have you ever thought what you do to your husbands with your expectations? There are many of you out there who are just like I was. When you married, you expected your husband to fill voids in your life that only God can fill. Take it from someone who has been there. If you ever expect someone other than God to give you security or significance, then you will always be very disappointed. Sad to say, many Christians walk around never having learned that lesson.

If you ever expect someone other than God to give you security
or significance, then you will always be disappointed.

Frank thought the way to be a good spiritual leader was to make me aware of all my wrong attitudes and actions and help me to confess them so I would be cleansed. He would tell me, "Barbara, that is sin and you need to confess it." All that would do was make me mad and I would just flaunt it.

The Bible instructs us to encourage and exhort one another, but ultimately the Holy Spirit is the one that convicts and changes people. The primary reason I did not receive Frank's exhortation with a teachable heart was that I did not feel loved by Frank. I felt more like his spiritual project than a wife whom he loved. Do you have a difficult person in your life? Instead of criticizing, try expressing love and encouragement to them. It may take some time, but God will use it in their lives, as well as yours.

In that miserable state, I lost all ability to pray. I hated being a hypocrite, but I was too low and depressed to do anything about it. I couldn't even read my Bible. All I felt was anger and bitterness and finally lost even the assurance of my salvation. Even lower than that, I wanted to take my life. This time the despair was very different from before when I wasn't a Christian — I knew that I would not be absorbed into the primal essence of life. There is a heaven and hell and I would end up in one or the other. Not knowing for sure if I were saved was the only thing that kept me from ending my life; if I really weren't a Christian, I knew I would go to hell.

One day in my desperation I fell down on my face on the den floor with three babies, Anita at 2½ years old, Frank III at 1½, and Peggy at ½, somewhere in the house. Looking back, I don't know where they were. An angel must have been babysitting. I cried out to God, "I can't take it anymore. I can't talk to You. I can't live with You. But I can't live without You. I'm miserable. You have to send me some help."

God heard my prayer and showed me two things that afternoon. First, from Jeremiah 2:13, *"'My people have committed two sins: they have forsaken me, the spring of living water, and have dug their own cisterns, broken cisterns that cannot hold water.'* You have forsaken Me, the Fountain of living water and you wonder why you're dying of thirst. When you had nothing, you found your total sufficiency in Me. But when I gave you Frank, you transferred all of your expectations to him. He was never designed to meet the need in your life that only I can. Come back to Me and let Me fill your life. Let your expectations be of Me." Deep down inside I understood what He was trying to show me.

Secondly, I imagined Adam in the Garden of Eden. God had told him to till the Garden and that was what Adam was doing. Then God said, *"It's not good for the man to be alone" (Genesis 2:18)*. So He sent him a helper to assist him in that which he was called to do. But Eve led him to the tree. It was like God said, "I brought Frank here to cultivate this part of My vineyard and I gave you to him to help him. But you came in and wanted to distract him and pull him away." It was like marriage fought with ministry. God was showing me that marriage was my ministry and I was to walk worthy of that calling, with all lowliness and meekness.

I broke under the loving, gentle hand of God that day and hours went by where I just communed with God. Pulling myself off the floor, I felt a new resurrection inside. As I sat back on the sofa, I picked up an Amplified New Testament that Frank had left there. Not looking for a particular verse, I flipped through it wondering what I could do now that I had surrendered to Him. I promise you, it just fell open to I Peter 3:2. I don't believe in "flip and dip" Bible study, but God flipped so I dipped. The verse describes how wives should reverence their husbands. It said that I was to *respect, defer to, revere him, to honor, esteem (appreciate, prize), and adore him which means to admire, praise, be devoted to, deeply love and enjoy.* It went on and on, none of which I did. I didn't even like him. The next thought that came was that obedience brings blessing. God doesn't call us to feel, but to do. So I asked the Lord to give me the strength to do two things out of that list. I would tell him I loved him, which I hadn't done in a long time, and I would praise him. If I began with two, maybe I could eventually work my way through the whole list.

I got my little speech together and waited for him to come home. He was late, as always, and my speech was getting colder and colder. I finally heard his car and planted myself at the back door. As he walked in, expecting the usual torrential outburst, I hurriedly said that I loved him and thought his sermon was wonderful. This wasn't his customary greeting and he nearly fell out the door.

At that same moment, something broke inside of me and suddenly I realized I did love him. I was glad he was a man of commitment and began seeing all of the other wonderful things about him.

Fortunately, about the same time, God began opening Frank's eyes to my needs and his legitimate responsibilities to me as his wife. I believe this marked the beginning of our Christian marriage. From that point on it was two steps forward and one step back, but at least we were headed in the right direction. I am so glad that God kept him blinded until I learned those very hard lessons.

Over the past forty years, I have sought to know God better and make Him known to others. Many times the spiritual lessons were learned the hard way, with much pain. What I would give to prevent you from repeating my same mistakes. If I could sit down with each of you for just a few minutes, I would love to pass on what I have learned. The following chapters were written with that desire in mind.

APPENDIX 2

MISCELLANEOUS FUN STORIES

Barbara, speaking of Briarwood Church:
"I think this is the greatest church
in the world. You might think
I'm prejudiced, but I'm not.
I've been around."

From Denise: The following are stories about Barbara that have no spiritual merit, but are entertaining and must be told. She reminds me of a Christian version of Lucy Ricardo.

HAWAII

After Frank and Barbara broke up, she was in Birmingham with nothing to do. So she taught English, Speech, and Drama at Mountain Brook Junior High, performing with Town and Gown in her spare time. Her heart was restless and she didn't know exactly what she wanted to do from a career perspective. That was the year Russia launched the rocket, Sputnik, and space travel was all anyone talked about. The American education system realized it needed to teach the next generation about aerospace, so they offered a course at the University of Hawaii. The summer course was directed specifically toward teachers who would go back to their schools and pass on what they learned. Being a pilot, Barbara was interested in space and rockets, plus she just wanted to get away. The group was housed at the Hawaiian Village Hotel on Waikiki Beach for that summer. The professors were Wernher von Braun, one of the leading pioneers in aerospace engineering, Edward Teller, developer of the hydrogen bomb, Kraft Ericky (the Mach 1 man), and Chuck Yeager, the first pilot to break the sound barrier.

Her assignment was to write a workbook to go along with a high-school textbook on aviation and rockets. The workbook took very complicated concepts and put them in language students could understand. You have to realize that her understanding of aviation was very limited; even though, she was a pilot. The farthest she had gotten with math was Algebra II in high school, majoring in Speech and Drama in college and minoring in English education. But she had purchased a children's book, *The Golden Book of Airplanes*, which spelled out the basic principles of thrust and aerodynamics. That little book, along with a lot of faking, is what got her through her pilot training.

Barbara will tell you that she never understood math, but one thing she remembered was that if the minus signs in an equation were an odd number, the equation had a negative value. While in Hawaii at one of the sessions with all of the rocket scientists, she came across an equation for rocket thrust in the textbook that these space-age experts had written. She noticed that there was an uneven number of negative signs and called her instructor's attention by saying, "Look at this equation. It looks like to me you would end up with vacuum and not thrust." Looking horrified, all of those international brains started working furiously over their figures. They worked and worked and finally told Barbara that she was right.

After that they treated her like she was a rocket scientist too, giving her all kinds of special privileges. As part of the course, the students got to go up an Air Force plane. Because she was already a pilot and knew the basic principles of flight, supposedly, they let her sit in the copilot seat and help fly the plane. She says this is how her whole life has been. She always knew just enough to impress somebody.

DIRECTING WEDDINGS

For years and years Barbara directed most of the weddings at Briarwood. She and Frank had it down to a science. He wouldn't even have to show up for the rehearsal on Friday night; she just told the bridal party everything they needed to know. For one particular June wedding, Frank was out of town for the weekend and one of the assistant ministers, Roland Travis, was scheduled to conduct the ceremony. When he didn't show up on Friday night, Barbara didn't think anything about it.

The next day at the wedding the mothers were seated, the music was playing, and Barbara was waiting in the church foyer with the bride. Right before the bridesmaids were to go down the aisle, one of the groomsmen came and said that the minister had not shown up. Barbara turned into a SWAT team commander. She sent one person to scour the audience looking for a substitute minister. Next, she instructed the groomsman to crawl on his hands and knees through the choir loft and tell the organist to keep playing. Then she went to the office to phone Roland. All this time the bride was in some kind of bridal bliss and never clued into the fact that they were in a crisis.

Roland's wife answered the phone and said he was down the street playing tennis; somehow, the wedding had not gotten on his calendar. Since Roland was in their only car, she sent their son on his bicycle to deliver black socks and shoes, with instructions for Roland to get to the church as fast as he could.

Back at the church, the organist had started on hymn one in the hymnbook and was proceeding on to hymn two, hymn three, etc. The mother of the bride was trying to be subtle in her attempts to see what was going on in the back of the church. And the bride was somewhere in la-la land, never even questioning the delay.

A substitute "minister" was found in the audience, but there was just a little problem. He was a seminary graduate who was not yet ordained. He kept arguing with Barbara that if he performed the ceremony it wouldn't be legal. That didn't faze her. In her sweet,

Scarlet O'Hara way, she said they would worry about that later.

Fortunately for everyone, Roland showed up before an illegal wedding took place. Barbara would say later that you would have never known that there was anything wrong except for the sweat pouring profusely from Roland's face and his hairy leg showing through the split in his robe every time he took a step.

GOING TO SLEEP

Barbara is famous in Briarwood circles for going to sleep any time she sits still. It really doesn't matter where it is, who she's with, or what she's doing. Everyone has just learned not to take it personally. Anybody that's ever spent any amount of time with her can tell you of an instance when they've been pouring out their heart to her and looked over to see her head bobbing. I'm really surprised that she doesn't have some kind of permanent neck injury.

For years she would sing in the choir. The newer members of the congregation would look up to the choir loft during the sermon to see her head bowed and think how godly the preacher's wife was in praying for her husband while he preached. We old-timers knew differently.

Barbara will tell you her sleeping is because she has narcolepsy; she was diagnosed. My personal opinion is that she never gets enough sleep. She only sleeps four or fives hours on a good night and it is not unusual for her to get less than that. Her phenomenal energy level would put anyone to shame. I've never known anyone that could keep up with her. We've learned not to even try.

Her "condition" is good for me in that she requires a driver when she speaks out of town. Frank laid down the law and told her she couldn't drive by herself longer than twenty minutes. Personally, I think that is pushing it. Anyway, I get the privilege of being one of her designated drivers. Every once in a while she will stay awake long enough to have brief conversations and I have learned so much from her. For the most part, this book is a result of those times.

She's told me a couple of her most embarrassing sleep moments. One occurred when Frank was moderator of the PCA General Assembly, which was held at in Philadelphia. In one of the sessions, while a young preacher was speaking, she was sitting in an old-timey, high-back wooden theatre seat fighting sleep. Right in the middle she snorted loudly as her head jerked back, knocking her noggin on the back of that wooden seat. The snort and crack were heard by people all around her.

The second instance was a prank by Randy Pope, the minister of Perimeter Presbyterian Church in Atlanta, when he and his wife, Carol, were visiting Frank and Barbara in Birmingham. Frank was scheduled to speak in a small PCA church in Brent, Alabama, so Barbara, Randy, and Carol went along to support him. As Frank was preaching, the other three sat on the front row and as usual Barbara went to sleep. Randy leaned over and whispered in Barbara's ear, "Barbara, Frank wants you to stand up." She quickly arose out of a dead sleep and proceeded to stand up and give one of those preacher wives' smiles — you know what I'm talking about, a cross between Queen Elizabeth in a parade and a movie star walking the red carpet. Before she could get to a standing position, Randy started pulling on Barbara's arm, telling her to sit down, that it was all a joke. Frank didn't know what to think; he just kept preaching.

FRANK TAKES A SLEEPING PILL ON THE PLANE TO KOREA

General Assembly of the PCA was in Fort Lauderdale one year and immediately after it was over, Frank and Barbara boarded a plane headed for South Korea, where Frank was scheduled to preach. They changed planes in Atlanta and weren't expected to get off the plane until they arrived in Seoul.

Frank always had difficulty sleeping on planes and knew he needed to rest for the grueling schedule ahead. He was in that too-exhausted-to-sleep state, so he took a sleeping pill as soon as they took off from Atlanta. After about thirty minutes, he was still wide awake so he took another one.

By the time they made an unexpected stop in Dallas, he was dead to the world. Unfortunately, the airline authorities made everyone leave the plane for some unknown reason. Try as she may, Barbara couldn't wake Frank up and the flight attendants were insistent that they get off. She pulled him into a standing (or should I say leaning) position and grabbed both of their big briefcases. No one volunteered to help her. She struggled to keep him on his feet, but all the way down the aisle of the plane and the jet way he was bumping into the seats and the walls.

When they got to the waiting area, Barbara was mortified at what everyone must be thinking. So she decided to make a little announcement to the crowd: "My husband isn't drunk. In fact, he's a minister and on his way to preach in Korea." At least one kind soul had mercy on them and helped get Frank back on the plane. Frank has no memory of the incident, except for walking into a wall.

From Denise: The next two stories have spiritual merit, but just don't fit well with any of the lessons. They are written as if Barbara is speaking.

SAYING NO TO FRANK

There was a time I reaped the consequences of not trusting God. Frank and I were asked to speak at a conference out of town. While we were there someone came up and handed us $20 and said to go out to eat. That was quite a treat, back in the days when $20 was a lot of money and money was much tighter. I couldn't wait to get back to Birmingham and indulge in a date with Frank. At the end of the conference, they took up an offering for missionaries and Frank leaned over and whispered to me to put the $20 bill in the offering plate. I told him, "No, I'm not going to do it. It was a gift to us and they wouldn't want us giving it away." He was not pleased. The offering plate came and went without a contribution from us.

When we got home and opened the door, we were overwhelmed with the smell of rotting meat. A young man living with us had accidentally left the freezer door open and all of our frozen meat had thawed and ruined. Therefore, the $20 was used to replace the freezer contents.

PINK FLUFFY TOWELS

Because I grew up in a rather affluent home, I sometimes had a hard time submitting to the sacrificial lifestyle Frank was determined we would have. In the early years he was not the loving, sensitive man he is today and would make me feel guilty for spending any money on myself. I felt he considered even lipstick a luxury. (But he might have reconsidered that if he had ever seen me without lipstick.) He would tell me, "Barbara, remember the dollar you are spending is the same dollar someone in our church sacrificed to give."

I was in Bromberg's one day getting my watch fixed and saw these beautiful pink towels on sale at a bargain price; they were almost giving them away. I really needed towels because I had not bought any since I married ten years before. My current ones were worn out from the three babies and all of those people who stayed at our house. There was never money to spend at will, but I thought I could swing buying them at that price. The clerk asked me if I wanted to have them monogrammed. When I married, monogramming was free, so not thinking it would be extra, I told her yes.

When the towels arrived, the bill for the monogramming was more than the towels themselves, far beyond what I could absorb in my small household budget. While trying to figure out how to pay for them, I went ahead and hung them in the bathroom, counting on the fact Frank never noticed anything. But that time he did.

The next day he asked me, "Honey, where did these towels come from?"

Thinking quickly, I blurted out, "A lady in the church wanted me to have them." It really wasn't a lie. A lady in the church did want me to have them. That lady just happened to be me.

He said, "Well, who was it?"

Whenever somebody in the church did something and didn't want to be recognized, Frank always said they wanted to remain unnamed. I thought that would work here, so I said, "She just wanted to remain unnamed."

He sweetly replied, "How nice."

My heart was so heavy, but I tried inside to justify my lie. After all, it was not a huge deal in the big scheme of life. Who really cared anyway? And besides, the towels would be used to minister to the people who stayed at our house. They would be ministry towels!

The next night I was trying to prepare my Bible study for the career girls' class and it just wasn't coming. Deep down I knew the reason was because I had deceived Frank. So I went and told him, "I was the lady in the church who wanted me to have the towels. I didn't want you to know because they cost more than I had planned."

He was so sweet and forgave me, adding, "Honey, have I made you feel so poor that you couldn't even buy towels?"

This story may seem trivial, but it was an important lesson for me, teaching me that because of God's Spirit living within me, I possess the power to say no to the temptations, like little white lies, that come along. And when I blow it, my fellowship with the Lord is broken. To restore it, I must go to Him and others quickly and ask forgiveness.

CPSIA information can be obtained at www.ICGtesting.com
Printed in the USA
LVOW11s1459160616

492898LV00001B/1/P